MW01107000

# Finding God
## Again and Again

John J. Spitzer, M.D.

ARCHWAY
PUBLISHING

Archway Publishing books may be ordered through booksellers or by contacting:

Archway Publishing
1663 Liberty Drive
Bloomington, IN 47403
www.archwaypublishing.com
844-669-3957

ISBN: 978-1-6657-0445-8 (sc)
ISBN: 978-1-6657-0443-4 (hc)
ISBN: 978-1-6657-0444-1 (e)

Library of Congress Control Number: 2021905232

Print information available on the last page.

Archway Publishing rev. date: 10/18/2021

# Contents

**Part 3**

There are groups of people to whom I would like to dedicate this book:

To my family—Anne, Tim, and Patty
You have been an inspiration to me and have helped me feel the love. We have had many happy times together, and you have helped me endure some of my more difficult times. You have been very much a major part of my journey.

To Father Fitz (Monsignor William Fitzgerald, 1931–2015)
You were my spiritual director, meeting with me almost monthly for a ten-year period prior to your passing. I often felt like I was talking to God in person, and I will always remember your expression of God holding you in His arms as you hugged yourself and smiled. I borrowed this gesture from you and used it in this book.

Anne introduced me to *The Road Back to You: An Enneagram Journey to Self-Discovery*,[1] by Ian Morgan Cron and Suzanne Stabile, as I was writing the final chapter for this book. I came to learn that I was a "number two," or the "helper," and my biggest sin to battle was pride. I was shocked at how well that chapter described me, and it made sense that the bulk of my book would be on the theme of pride and humility. So to all of you number twos, I dedicate this book to you as well.

Finally, I dedicate this work to the Triune God. I am simply a messenger, and nothing would make me happier than to know that this book is of help to those who are on their journey toward God.

# Introduction

> Through money and power, you
> cannot solve all problems.
> The problem in the human heart
> must be solved first.
> —His Holiness the Dalai Lama
> *Kindness, Clarity, and Insight*

In 1998, I found out I was having a relapse of testicular cancer after being cancer-free for thirteen years. I have to admit I was very scared because having cancer relapses meant the disease had been spreading at a microscopic level before it was detected by our current conventional medical methods, and who knows where it had decided to seed? There was a sense of failure associated with this; a failure that meant my life was at risk. My wife and I had battled together my first bout with cancer in 1985, but now, I had two children, ages five and two. I was scared for my young family and the challenges they would have without me.

My initial response in 1985 to finding out that I had cancer was a philosophical and religious one. I was in medical school and in my midtwenties. I thought my faith in God was strong, and if I was going to die, then it was God's will. This was quickly changed into feelings of anger and desire for control as I went through surgeries and chemotherapy—a survival response, if you will. By the time I was done with all my treatments, I felt I could actually will life for myself, and I could make events happen. I could run and play soccer whenever I wanted to. I could remain healthy and strong if I wanted to. I was full of energy; I had friendships; I could smile; I felt love. There was nothing that could stop me unless I consented for that to happen.

And then, after thirteen years of being cancer-free, I got hit again. Cancer had decided to come back, and I found myself going through denial, which I never did the first time in 1985. I experienced a deeper fear of losing my life. Having a cancer relapse meant that everything I went through, including the three surgeries and three months of intense chemotherapy in 1985, all had failed. And so here I was in 1998, facing what seemed like impending death. How was it possible that after thirteen years of being cancer-free, this ugly thing could come back? I feared for Anne and the kids. Anyone who has been a parent knows how difficult it is to raise children, to give them a proper education about life, where you hope to install in them a good set of values and help sculpt their characters so that they one day can carry the family baton for you. I felt this huge job would fall on Anne's shoulders, and although I am still 100 percent confident that she would do an outstanding job without me, there is no doubt that the job would be easier with me around, another helping hand.

As if one relapse with cancer was not bad enough, I got hit again in the year 2000. But this time, my perspective on cancer relapses was different because I let go. Although I had always been very religious, this last relapse certainly turned out to be a great opportunity to become one with God.

I can remember when I was about twelve years old, and I felt a strong pull to go to church on my own. Having grown up in a Catholic family, I went through the sacraments, like all other Catholics do: baptism, reconciliation, confession, penance, first Communion, and confirmation. I remember well my first Communion at the age of eight. I felt very special and privileged to be closer to God. But it wasn't until I was twelve years old that I found myself craving to go to church on my own. There was tremendous wisdom to be had at church, and I wanted that. I wanted to make myself a better person. I wanted to help people, and I wanted to channel this energy in the right direction. With my family, I helped poor people by supplying them with food and clothing. In high school, I taught children at an orphanage in reading and mathematics. I could feel the energy and love in my heart.

But as I grew older, I became more educated and improved in my thinking skills. Two religion classes that I had in college made an impact on my faith, and thus, the teachings from the church and from my Catholic schooling made more sense. What subsequently happened was that the initial calling from God, which seemed to be mainly a feeling about God in my heart, was replaced by one with a lot of theory and rationalization. Don't get me wrong. The intellectual information was important to build a better faith in God, but it took me a little over twenty years of life experiences to realize again that I had to feel God in my heart again and not just think of God. I had to feel Jesus and his teachings if I wanted to be like him.

This change in my relationship with God—from one that was based on thinking and reasoning to one that was based on my feelings for God in my heart—paralleled my change in my will for life from 1985 to 2000. My will for life in 1985 was initially selfish, stubborn, and driven by me, whereas in 2000, it began to change to one of quietness and was driven by God. My will did not have to be put aside or given up; rather, my will could fall in line with God's will. There was less anxiety and less stress if my will conformed to God's will. As the perceptions about my will changed, I actually started to crave dying. Death felt peaceful and joyful. I wanted to be one with God. It then almost seemed like a paradox: to will life and death at the same time.

When I first embarked on writing this book in September 2001, I did it mainly because I thought I might die and wanted to leave to my children some knowledge about life, in particular as it related to God. Seven months later, by April 2002, I had written the first eight chapters of the book fairly fast, even sometimes waking up in the middle of the night to write. However, I found myself still alive in 2007 and wondered what I was going to do with this book. Since my prayerful life and relationship with God continued to change during that five-year span, I decided to start writing again in 2007. I had met Father Fitz in 2005, and he was gracious enough to become my spiritual director. He also encouraged me to continue writing, more from the point of view of self-discovery and using the writing to help improve my relationship with God, while not letting myself become attached to the writings. We met almost monthly for about ten years, until he passed away in 2015. To this day, I still miss our monthly meetings. What followed were a number of chapters describing my spiritual development until 2019, when I felt it was time to finish this project. I had been wondering, prior to 2019, if I should publish it or not, as I continued to put out chapters but found myself thinking about it too much, which made me realize I was becoming attached to the book. I made the decision to let go of the book, and if it was helpful to people, then it was God's will.

I decided to break up the book into three parts, as the writings became pretty different. In part 1, written between 2001 and 2002, I wrote the first eight chapters from memory as to how my life had evolved since my childhood. It was a pretty factual account of past events, as I discussed the beginning of my relationship with God and the development of daily prayer. Part 2, written from 2007 to 2018, was more contemporary and related to the present events in my life as they related to God at the time. This section reflects the struggles I had in the development of my relationship with God, as sometimes I felt close to God; at other times, I struggled for that intimacy. The short writings took place at different times as I saw them from my own time, but I think that for God, these were just struggles along a continuum without time. Because my prayer style changed during this time, my writing style also changed. The final section, part 3, written between 2019 and 2020, reflects my coming to peace with God in my heart, acknowledging God's love, and acknowledging God as my all, to whom I longed to return, to my true home. In God's divine providence, my wife has been with me all along and has been a rock for me. Thus, part 3 begins with the acknowledgment that God has been working through her and helping us share God's love for each other.

I would say two factors influenced a change in my style of writing as I went from part 1 to part 2 of the book: my prayer life changed and became more contemplative. I learned to just rest in God's arms and feel God's love and peace. And second, I have read several books by Father James Martin and love his style of writing. More profoundly, my relationship with Jesus changed after I read Father Martin's book, *Jesus, A* Pilgrimage,[2] published in 2014. I used to see Jesus as God, perfect in every way but distant from me. Jesus was high up, and I was down here. After reading the book, I found myself developing a relationship with Jesus, and I have learned a lot from him. I gained a new appreciation for reading the Gospels, in particular the Gospel according to John. Father James's discourse on the Jesuit style of praying allowed me to incorporate imagery into my prayer, such that my chapters toward the end of the book reflect this style of praying and writing.

My perception of God also changed as I went into the second part of the book. The Old Testament writings that I read in grade school and high school created in me a vision of a God who was demanding, strong, masculine, and stern. This understanding and attitude permeated my writings in part 1. As I developed a relationship with Jesus during part 2, I began to appreciate that God is very kind, gentle, merciful, and compassionate. I was then able to put in perspective and understand better those writings in the Old Testament, where God was coming across as stern and demanding, yet with compassion and love.

In addition to changing my view of God as a strong father figure up in the sky, I began to see God in a nongender form and was unable to use words to describe God's essence but was able to feel love and peace from God. The reader will likely notice that I avoided gender-specific pronouns when referencing God, and it some paragraphs, the use of *God* may seem redundant.

My faith and my spiritual development have been through the Catholic faith and church. Thus, a lot of my writing will reflect this teaching. However, I have come to appreciate that the development of our relationship with God comes in many forms, from different spiritualities within the Catholic Church, such as the Franciscan way to the Jesuit way or the Carmelite way, to different religions that are Protestant, Jewish, or Islamic, to name a few. I believe that at the end of the day, what is most important is that we acknowledge that we are spiritual beings; we have souls that God created, and we return to God when we are done with this earthly life.

The physician in me and my scientific way of thinking has led me to put dates at the top of the chapters when I wrote them. These dates create a time span during which I changed spiritually. I have come to appreciate that spiritual change takes time, and sometimes it can be decades, as it has been for me. What I have found in my spiritual development is that I often hit a plateau in prayer and in my relationship with God after having a stressful event. This stressful event resulted in some struggle spiritually, but then, I came out the other end with more peace and love. These plateaus lasted months to years before I encountered another event that then challenged me spiritually before I hit another plateau. As a consequence, in looking at part 2, the time span in between chapters varied, depending on when I hit my next spiritual challenge, which then led to another plateau.

I have used the New International Version Bible and the Bible Gateway as a reference tool from HarperCollins Christian Publishing, Inc., whenever I quoted any readings from the Bible and from Jesus.

I talk about my childhood years in the 1970s, while in Colombia, South America. With the utmost respect, I briefly talk about the struggles the country went through after that time period. It pleases my heart, as I write this introduction in 2020, to see the country getting back to better stability. In addition, I have enjoyed watching the Colombian national soccer team do so well at the international level.

I believe that in the depths of our hearts, we have two main yearnings: we yearn to find who we are, hopefully to find out we are as God made us to be; and we yearn for love, hopefully realizing that it is God's love we are looking for.

This book has been about self-discovery, finding out who I am as God made me to be. Deep in my heart, there is this yearning to find out who I am, even if I sometimes can't put that yearning into words. Working on this discovery and finding out about my talents, as God sees fit to use my talents in God's divine providence, peace, and satisfaction, sink in deep in my heart. This state of peace is fueled by God's love, as God loves me just the way I am. But better yet, God loves the person I am yet to become, more so than the person that I am currently. It feels to me like God is jumping up and down with excitement as I get closer to becoming who I am supposed to be. There is confidence in my heart in this belief because God has made me in God's image, and God wants to see me realize myself completely as God created me, in my potential capacity.

This journey of self-discovery does not happen in isolation but in relationship with God and with all the people who surround me, with all of life's complexities and with all the pain and sufferings but also with all the joyful moments and acts of love. To paraphrase Pope Benedict XVI from his book, *Benedictus, Day by Day*,[3] it is in our relatedness with God that we begin to discover ourselves as God meant for us to be. As I draw closer to God, I begin to feel God's love and God's arms wrapping around me and telling me, "You are my beloved son, with whom I am well pleased." Then I can begin to rest quietly in God's love.

And this book also has been about finding God's love. Life's struggles have given me an opportunity to feel God's love and mercy.

It is in this state of God's love and allowing God to flow through me that my heart begins to change so that I can reach out to the world and take care of people—God's love to people as it flows through me. When I care for the other in a humble and meek manner, as Jesus taught us in the Sermon on the Mount, then I can begin to make our world a better place to live. Jesus did not use political power or money to effect change; rather, he used love with humility and meekness as it flowed freely from his heart, without any physical or emotional attachments.

Being able to let this love flow freely from my heart requires that I know myself and that I discover what impedes the flow of love from my heart. Then, as I look at all the problems we face today, I can set aside my material, emotional, and spiritual attachments and care for the other with freedom in my heart to impart peace, mercy, and love. It is at this point, I believe, that I can then do my part in making our world a better place to live.

# Part 1

Part I

# Chapter 1

# Life Is a Dance

## *June 2001*

I t is June 21, 2001, and I can't think of anything more romantic today than dancing the foxtrot to Frank Sinatra. While keeping our backs straight and our shoulders up and flexed at right angles, we maintain our arms extended and the elbows partly flexed. We keep good muscle tone to maintain dancing posture and provide a good connection between our bodies. With our heads slightly extended and tilted to our right, we begin to dance. The smooth gliding of our felt-soled dance shoes on this imported, fine wood dance floor from Denmark gives life to the room as we move gracefully from one end to the other. First, a basic forward, then some chain steps, followed by promenade walks, with and without underarm turns. Our eyes are fixed on each other as if falling in love for the first time. Junior walks and forward promenades conclude our dance as we head into a waltz. It is gracefulness, as if floating on air. The one-two-three beat takes us across the room with Viennese turns, forward and backward chain steps, and forward promenades. We finish in the center of the room with a series of right and left underarm turns, as I display her beauty to nobody else but me—with a left rock turn as I bring her body across mine from my right side on a ninety-degree turn; with a corkscrew turn to watch her head tilt even more gently as I contemplate her green-hazel eyes, her beautiful long eyebrows, and her soft lips; and finally, with a graceful side step and a left underarm turn to end the dance.

It is hard to believe that we are celebrating today another wedding anniversary. Anne has been the love of my life, and we have been there for each other through thick and thin. We have been surprising each other over the span of three days with a series of events. Today's surprise was Anne's, as she had reserved the studio for lunchtime. A wonderfully cooked meal by one of our friends was followed by ballroom dancing. Our instructor was kind enough to accommodate Anne's wish to reserve the studio at lunchtime. Much to our amusement, I had surprised Anne two days earlier with ballroom dancing at another location that was used primarily for aerobics.

I never would have envisioned, at the age of forty, that ballroom dancing would be such a big part of my life. Although it is very athletic and, in fact, considered an Olympic event at this time, I define myself better as a runner and a soccer player. But I gave up soccer four years ago because of injuries. My last injury—a broken right leg and a sprained ankle—left me walking away from the sport that I had played for twenty-eight years. The dancing that plays out in soccer seems similar to that in ballroom dancing, but it is more physical. The sidestep to the right, the dribble to the left, the forward fake with the shoulders, and the Brazilian motion of the hips, as I wait for the defender to commit in one direction so that I can go to the other side. That is the beauty of soccer, and I owe that style of play to my years in Colombia, South America.

As I sit down to rest after a number of dances and quench my thirst with a drink of water, I begin to look back at my life and how it evolved over the years. You could say that I am from the East Coast, since I was born in New Jersey in 1961. My accent, however, makes it difficult for people to tell where I am from. My dad is a Wisconsin native with German and Irish heritage. He lived in New York and New Jersey for many years, however, and his accent is more Eastern than Midwestern. His speech influence, combined with my Colombian Spanish, gives me a different way of pronouncing words. For the most part, my English is pretty smooth, but when I get tired, my syntax sometimes takes on a Spanish flare, or sometimes, I simply mispronounce words.

I was born in Salem, New Jersey, and attended kindergarten before I went to Cali, Colombia, at the age of six. I remember some peaceful times in Salem, like spending time with Mom in the kitchen, baking cookies together and trying to learn some Spanish words in anticipation that maybe, someday, we would travel to Colombia. I also remember the sense of security I felt when we visited my grandmother Agnes Spitzer (née Murphy), a strong Irish lady with a deep faith in God. I later learned that she taught Mom a lot about parenting. She always seemed to have the right answer. Grandma Murphy, as we called her, knew when it was time to play with the soldiers and forts, when it was time to play outside, and when it was time to cuddle and read. As I grew into my teenage years, our games progressed to board games and card games. In particular, she loved to play gin rummy. Her praying by herself in her room in the afternoon before dinner left me with a big impression about the routine and importance of prayer.

Everybody on Mom's side of the family resided in Colombia. After I turned six years old, we all moved to Cali, Colombia, including my two younger brothers, but not my father. Although my father would visit us once or twice a year, Mom and Dad's relationship eventually weakened and ended up in divorce when I was nineteen years old.

My initial impression of Colombia was one of disbelief. The surroundings were different, and everybody spoke a language that I could not understand. We had lived in a suburban area in New Jersey, with ample space in between houses and each house with a grass lawn, but houses in Cali were close to each other, and it was easy to sometimes hear neighbors over the walls. I was insecure and was attached to my mom's leg for quite some time. But my relatives were nice and always had smiles on their faces. They were just as amused that I could speak a different language from theirs. As I warmed up to them, we began to ask each other for translations: "How do you say this in Spanish?" or "What does this mean in English?" It became a fun game and helped ease my transition to a new life.

First grade in Cali was a challenge. I was fortunate that my teacher knew English, so this eased the transition of learning a second language while I learned a new culture. Latin American people are very affectionate. Personal space is invaded often with a hug, a shoulder-to-shoulder bump, touching on the arm, or simply standing close by. Eye contact and reading the other person's facial expression is an ongoing process. You learn to speak a nonverbal language from very young, and later, it can be complimentary or misleading to the verbal language and can create miscommunications.

At that time, in the late '60s and early '70s, Cali had about 800,000 people, but it has grown now to about two million. The city sits in the southwest part of Colombia, in between the Andes Mountain ranges, or *cordilleras*, of the west and central, in a valley at a height of about 3,300 feet. The houses were all connected to each other; only walls of plaster separated one house from the other. Gardens and trees did not color the city unless you lived in the outskirts and in wealthy areas. As the climate was fairly tropical, the houses were open to fresh air all the time, with open-ceiling patios in the middle of the house.

Most of the time, it was nice to have the sun shining through the windows and the breeze carrying its fresh scent from the mountains. But the inside of our house often got wet when it rained hard. It would be even worse when the house would flood, along with the streets, during the tropical rain season. As kids, however, we would always find a way to entertain ourselves in the rain, like attempting to play soccer on a water-filled street. Even funnier yet, sometimes we would run barefoot in almost knee-deep brown water, with brooms in hand, while chasing rats as they were evacuated from their sewer homes.

School was hard, but it was expected that everybody would study hard. It was a system that did not make exceptions for children with learning disabilities or attention problems. If they did not perform well academically, they would be retained. If students did not study or do their homework, they would get poor grades and consequently be retained. Most schools were Catholic, whether public or private. I initially attended a public school but later transferred to a private Franciscan high school. We attended mass once a week at school and said the prayer of Saint Francis every morning. Coed schools were rare. I attended an all-boys school, which really made us look forward to the weekend dances when I was in high school. Discipline by the priests was very strict, but this was a continuation of the discipline methods and expectations by parents. There was a lot of emphasis in the culture to be obedient, polite, and thankful.

Not everything was gloomy and rigid, however. People in Cali knew how to have fun. In fact, back in those days, *los caleños*, as people from the other Colombian cities would call us, liked to party all the time. People enjoyed dancing, and you could count on a dance party almost every weekend. From salsa to merengue and from rumba to cha-cha, the styles of dancing flowed through our bloodstreams. Parties would start around nine or ten at night and last until two or four in the morning. Sometimes, we would be so hungry and thirsty afterward that we would hit a restaurant or diner in the early morning to get a tamale, empanada, or hamburger, with a tall glass of Coke.

We did learn how to drink alcohol early on in our lives. Beer was not very popular, but we drank aguardiente, or "hot water," which was about 80 proof and could knock your socks off. We walked everywhere we went, so drinking and driving was not an issue. I have to admit that I had some pretty good hangovers when I was in high school, between fourteen and seventeen years of age. Waking up in the afternoons was common on the weekends.

If we were not dancing, we were playing soccer. It was hard to play during the school week because we were doing our homework and studying, but the streets would be filled with soccer stars on the weekend—at least we thought we were soccer stars. We were always trying to emulate the next star. Sometimes it was an Argentinean or Brazilian, and sometimes it was somebody from our own Colombian home turf. I particularly became attached to our right wing, a native Colombian whose dribbling moves and speed left defenses in the dust. I happened to be in Cali during a time when our home soccer team did very well. Deportivo Cali won the national championship four times from 1967 to 1974. Sometimes, we would play just one game a day on the streets, small-sided games such as four-on-four, with rocks for goals. During the World Cups, however, we could sometimes play three pickup games in a day. What else was there to wish for when you could play soccer all day? I often listened to the games on my transistor radio, but I could hear the crowd roar when our team scored, as the soccer stadium, Pascual Guerrero, was just five blocks away from home. It was better yet when Mom sometimes gave me money, and I would walk to the stadium with my friends to watch a game. Deportivo Cali was my team, and I loved their green jerseys and white shorts.

I have very fond memories of Cali and Colombia. The country was relatively stable back then, and the economy was hanging in there. The Colombian coffee bean was rated number one in quality, although Brazil was a bigger producer. The city had held the Pan American games in 1971, and I was very proud to be an American as I saw the USA sweep many events. It made an impression on me that I so often heard the United States national anthem after an American won the gold medal. I had firsthand experience as a ten-year-old Cub Scout, since I worked at the track-and-field venue, carrying the athletes' warmups from one end to the other. It was always fun to speak in English to the American and Canadian athletes.

Drugs of abuse were not an issue for us, although the country already had developed a reputation at an international level for supplying the United States and other countries with cocaine and marijuana. There were bands of guerillas located out in the country and farmland, and every so often, they would spray-paint slogans on walls to let people know they existed. But I never felt threatened by them, and everybody led a normal life. Politics pretty much went back and forth between the conservatives and the liberals, but the extreme right or left wings were not present. It is sad today to see the Colombian society struggle internally because of the political corruption, the drug cartels, and the unstable economy.

As I look at my life in Colombia and I compare it to what other children experience today in the United States, I find that I experienced problems not much different from what other children may have experienced. Without my father's presence in the family, I found myself in a position, as a child, of being the man of the house, since I was the oldest. My most demanding and difficult job was trying to help Mom raise my two younger brothers. I also helped with daily routine care, such as cooking, washing clothes, and cleaning the floors. For the most part, I was happy to help ease Mom's burden. The part of the job that I detested the most—and certainly did not do a good job of it, now that I can look back as a parent of two children—was being put in a parental role to discipline my two younger brothers. There were a lot of arguments and yelling. I felt like I was growing up in a hurry and was not ready for that, but I didn't know any better and didn't have the wisdom to change the course.

I think the most challenging problem I faced, mainly when I was between thirteen and seventeen years old, was dealing with my mom's alcoholism. Life became stressful for her during those years, as her marriage weakened and she felt her support system gradually dissolve. My aunts and uncles were always involved, but they also had their own families to take care of. Mom gradually pulled away from life, and my role as a "parent" became bigger. To escape from our family problems, I often went to our terrace on the third floor to lie in the sun and rest. I would daydream about hockey and soccer, and frequently, I would become quiet in my head and in my heart, just being there and finding some peace.

Many times, when I was not able to deal with the stress and pain of being at home, I would just walk away. I cried often, either in my room or out at the Olympic park, where many people would walk by, although it seemed that nobody noticed—at least I thought nobody noticed. I had many talks with God about my sufferings and asked for help, but I often felt that God was not listening to me, and I felt very lonely. My escape from the stressful life became playing soccer and roller hockey. Being home meant working as a parent while still trying to grow up and studying hard so I could get good grades.

After many years, however, both my mom and dad changed for the better. Mom became a recovering alcoholic when she came back to the United States. Her relationship with God improved dramatically through her daily prayer, going to church, and simply helping out at church with activities that benefited the people in need. Of all the qualities that I admire in her, I admire her humility the most. This quality was always present wherever she went, and I am sure she learned a lot from our Blessed Mother Mary, the humblest of all creatures, with whom she prayed often.

My father also learned a lot about life, and interestingly enough, now that he is in his sixties, his relationship with God also has improved a fair amount. He has come to appreciate the value of daily prayer, a special gift from God. I visit with my parents every so often, and I am pleased and thankful that my relationship with them has changed for the better.

My relationship with my brothers also has improved, and I have come to appreciate them as adults with their own families. I look back at these changes and appreciate them as gifts from God. As I encountered cancer and experienced God's love and mercy, I appreciated better how God can work on our hearts and change us for the better.

# Chapter 2

# Dealing with Cancer

*September 2001*

I t is the summer 1985, and I am having a dream. I feel weightless, and I am suspended in space, with many stars engulfing me, as if I belong here. The surroundings are pitch-black, except for the flickering of lights from these faraway twinkles. It is very quiet, and I am thoughtless. I am not even interested as to why I am here, but I am certainly curious as to what is about to happen. A small-capsule, wingless spaceship slips from underneath me as it invites me to enter and take a seat. As if I am a puppet, I am dropped in this ship, and the hatch closes. This is a one-seat vessel, very compact, with enough room for only one person. As I sit with my knees slightly flexed and my back a bit reclined, I grab the wheel and wait for my next command. There are no controls in this ship, no gadgets, no infrared lights, and no meters. Without any further actions, I pause and contemplate for a moment how comfortable I feel and how well I can see myself, despite the darkness that surrounds me.

I develop a firmer grip on the wheel as the ship begins to move forward. I don't see a destination, but my eyes are locked into the future. This is an unknown destination. What waits for me? Will somebody be there for me? As I pick up speed, the ship begins to shake and rumble, and I wonder if this craft was made to handle high velocities. I have no way of stopping this ship; in fact, the ship shakes and rumbles even more as it picks up more speed, and I fear that it might break into millions of pieces.

"Just hang on, John. You are going to be OK; just hang on." I grab the wheel tighter as my feet press hard against the floor and my back is firm against the seat. The feeling is overwhelming as I dash through space at the fastest speed known to humankind. This sensation lasts a few seconds, but it seems to be an eternity. Finally, I pop into a beautifully bright sky—I can't keep my eyes open for long because the light is too bright. The rumbling and shaking are gone, and I find myself suspended in air without a ship, weightless and amazed. After a brief moment of peacefulness and contentment, I wake up from my dream. My sheets are drenched, and I feel hot and sweaty as I stare at the bedroom ceiling.

It is sometime in the middle of the night, and I find myself in awe of this dream I've just had. The feeling of speed was a great sensation, but what was this dream about? Why did I have to hang on so hard?

I was diagnosed with testicular cancer three weeks ago, toward the end of my second year of medical school. We had just learned to examine genitals in our second year, and we had been encouraged to examine our own. Oddly enough, in November 1984, during my own exam, there seemed to be a lump in one of my testicles. A resident physician thought it was an infection and gave me an antibiotic. There were no associated symptoms at that time to go along with that lump.

That tiny lump never went away, but I felt healthy, as I was in good physical shape from running and playing soccer and basketball. I denied that this could be a tumor until it became more obvious, six months later, that there had to be a better explanation for why the right side of my scrotum was twice as large as the left side. I had developed some lower back pain, which I attributed to exercise and sports, but I could always get temporary relief from Advil. I saw a different resident physician in May 1985, who sent me to a urologist; I saw him the next day.

The tone of denial began to weaken as I was confronted with a reality that maybe I did have tumor. But final exams for the second semester were coming up the following week, and my fighting spirit soon went into high gear. It was the end of May, and the freshness in the air invigorated me. Nothing was going to stop me from finishing my second year!

I met the urologist on a Tuesday, a well-respected surgeon in the community. He was impressed that I was a medical student and treated me as if I were his colleague. I appreciated his sense of comfort and his sense of humor, but all he needed was a quick physical examination, and his facial expression changed to one of concern.

"John, I am afraid you have a tumor and a hydrocele [sac of water] to explain the swelling in your scrotum. We can do surgery on Thursday and find out what is going on."

Was I going to have surgery in thirty-six hours? Who turned the fan on high and made my hair stick straight up? That certainly didn't leave me with much time to do anything else. I called my dad and Anne, whom I was going to marry the following year. I did not call my mom, as she was still in Colombia, and I didn't want to worry her prematurely. I also talked to some of my classmates that night, and I appreciated their support. But fear very gradually began to creep in, and I felt a loss of control. I was about to embark on something I had never done before—general anesthesia and surgery. Was it true that some people did not wake up from general anesthesia? Who could reassure me that I would wake up from general?

I had a restless sleep that night but did go to class the next day, on Wednesday. It was amazing how quickly Thursday morning came around, and just like that, I found myself in a hospital room in a blue gown and with a blue cap to cover my hair. The feeling of bare skin on that starch-coated gown, with ample room for cool breezes through the back, was the beginning of many unusual experiences. My feelings in the operating room were ambivalent: excited since I was going into the medical profession but scared because I was about to be cut open.

The staff was very nice, smiling, and talkative. I listened without saying much initially, as I tried to absorb what was going on as much as possible. As I relaxed, I began to answer their questions regarding medical school and what field I might end up practicing. Once I got going with sharing my thoughts and feelings, I could not stop talking. The anesthesiologist told me that the sedative he was about to inject was going to make me sleepy. Not knowing what would happen, I waited while I continued to talk. My eyelids got heavy and they closed shut, despite my desire to keep them open. The nurses chuckled as I continued to talk as if I was not going to go to sleep. I refused to lose control but wanted to be polite about it. Finally, the second dose of the sedative came, and all I remember was somebody saying, "See you in recovery, John."

After waking up with a metallic taste in my mouth in the recovery room, I went to the surgical floor, where I recovered quickly over the next twenty-four hours and was discharged back to my apartment. I took my final exams and finished my second year. The battle of the big C, however, was just beginning, as I quickly had a CT scan of my abdomen and chest that revealed cancer metastasis in my retroperitoneum, an area in the abdomen behind my intestines but in front of my spine. The lymph nodes in this area had been infiltrated with cancer, but my chest was clear. This explained the back pain I had been having as these lymph nodes along either side of my spine had gotten bigger. The pathology report from the removed testicle showed a mixed-cell type of tumor: choriocarcinoma, embryonal cell carcinoma, seminoma, and yolk sac tumor.

I pulled the books out again and began to read madly about my disease. Frightening thoughts raced through my head as I read some of the statistics: 5 percent survival rate for choriocarcinoma;

15 percent survival rate for embryonal carcinoma; seminoma had a better prognosis. What about if you were to mix all of these in one case? Was the survival worse? I worried deeply for my life and my life with Anne. I struggled with the thoughts of how someone dies from cancer. Was it painless? Do you throw up a lot? What makes you throw up? Maybe this was the end of the road for me.

I became philosophical about life and started to retrieve some of my religious beliefs. I'd had an adventuresome life, with all its ups and downs. I felt thankful for my life, and it was now time to go back to God. *Isn't this what life is all about?* I thought. *When the call comes, I just have to humble myself and give thanks.*

That's right; time to give thanks and praise. Take me as I am, Lord. I am all yours, and I am thankful to you for giving me an opportunity to learn about life and to experience the world. I am thankful for the people you have put me in touch with. I am thankful that you let me get into medical school, although I was not one of the better students in the classroom. I did excel in the hospital and clinics, and I am thankful for that. I am thankful that you brought me back to the United States and gave me a second wind. I am thankful for meeting Anne. I am thankful that you let me play hockey and soccer.

I kept my feelings hidden, as I did not want to come across as a quitter. My feelings became ambivalent, as one side of me was ready to gently throw in the towel, and the other wanted to fight, mainly for Anne and my family. If I were to die, their pain would be my pain. How could I mix peacefulness with pain? I decided to follow the medical advice from my urologist to see a specialist, with whom he was familiar from his residency training, since I still did not have all the answers to my problem.

Two weeks later, I went to Indianapolis to meet Dr. Lawrence Einhorn. I was scheduled for a second surgery there to have all that metastasis removed from my retroperitoneum. Depending on the pathology reports from this metastasis, I might need to have chemotherapy. I'd never had chemotherapy before so that made this another new experience. What is it about chemotherapy that makes you feel so sick? Why do you throw up, and why do you lose your hair? *I guess I'll cross that bridge when the time comes.*

General anesthesia seemed less intimidating the second time around in Indianapolis. A procedure that was going to last about six hours turned into a two-hour case. Apparently, there was too much metastasis for surgical excision, and some of my nodes appeared to be embedded in my inferior vena cava. Chemotherapy, hopefully, would be able to shrink some of the mass and make surgery easier the next time, as this was, at the time, still considered somewhat unchartered territory.

Whereas waking up from general surgery the first time around seemed like a piece of cake, this second time around felt more intrusive. Although I had been given information about what I would have attached to me when I woke up from anesthesia, I still felt like my body had been violated, and I wanted to fight back. I had the endotracheal tube still in my airway as I was waking up. There was a nasogastric tube coming from my stomach and sticking out my nose. There were two internal jugular IVs in my neck, one on each side. I had a regular IV line in my right hand and an arterial line in my left wrist, which helped the anesthesiologist monitor my blood pressure and blood gases while I was on the ventilator during surgery. I had a Foley catheter sticking out from my penis, and two inflatable bags were wrapped around my legs, squeezing them every so often to avoid my developing blood clots in my legs while I lay in bed.

I was disappointed that surgery had not been more successful. I wanted the tumor and cancer to be gone. I wanted to feel free and untangled from this whole mess. But reality ruled my life at the moment. I had had major surgery and needed to recover. There was definitely more pain involved with this recovery. I had a zipper line right down the middle of my abdomen, from the tip of my breastbone to the top of the pubic bone, that was very sensitive to movement. Coughing made the pain excruciating. Gradually, over

14

the days, I began to increase my activity, first tolerating just being able to sit by the bedside, to then standing up and then, eventually, walking.

I met Dr. Einhorn and one of his fellows around my fifth day postoperative. I couldn't believe how confident they felt that my cancer could be cured! The survival statistics they quoted me were so different from those that I had read in my pathology book. Their facial expressions were serene but determined. They outlined a plan for chemotherapy as if there were no other options. This was the new protocol, and it had been very successful for others.

I struggled once more with my spirituality. The renewed confidence that I developed after talking with Dr. Einhorn gave me energy to leave the hospital on post-op day seven. I was to start chemotherapy the following Monday, which meant that I only had a four-day weekend for pleasure before taking these medicines. *Surprise! I am going to live!*

That fighting energy that I experienced from waking up from my second surgery, along with Dr. Einhorn's confidence, set the tone for the rest of the summer.

What do you mean that I was going to die? Who was talking about giving me up and glorifying God? Certainly not me! I am going to live! I felt like a fight was starting inside of me, but I couldn't tell if this fight was going to be against God or if it was just my survival instinct.

This chemotherapy plan was well structured, and it made sense. There would be twelve weeks of chemotherapy, four blocks of three weeks each. During the first week of each block, I would be hospitalized and get all three chemotherapy agents: cisplatinum, etoposide, and bleomycin. The next two weeks would consist of weekly outpatient visits, where I would get additional bleomycin. I felt more invigorated than ever, and I was determined to beat this cancer. I actually felt a little mad, maybe because I thought God was testing my faith and I did not want to be tested.

I came home after the hospital with this kind of mad attitude. It was the kind of mad and determined attitude that I sometimes had when playing soccer games, where I played well and scored many goals. My plans for the weekend were to visit Anne and her family, trying to get away, both physically and mentally, before embarking on this battle. I never envisioned that night that I would have one of the more powerful dreams ever. Hanging on to the steering wheel of a spaceship, I would hear somebody say to me, "Just hang on, John. You are going to be OK." Deep down, I wanted to believe that God was talking to me, but I was too mad at God at the time. Maybe it was a relative of mine who had passed away. Either way, this gave me a deeper sense of confidence that I was going to be cured. All I needed to do was to hang on!

# Chapter 3

# Chemotherapy and God's Messengers

*October 2001*

It was early June 1985, and the morning sun was piercing the windows in our living room. My head did not feel fogged up that morning as I sat on the sofa, reading the *Chicago Tribune*. The white walls lit up the room and added life to the day. My dad's condominium was a two-bedroom place on the second floor. You could tell that three guys lived here because our decor was very simple and practical. We had a couple of large contemporary art pictures on the walls, and the curtains were solid beige. The entertainment cabinet was simulated oak and held our TV and stereo. My brother Bob did a great job configuring the stereo system with the TV so that it seemed like we had a surround-sound theater. Both Bob and Dad had gone to work, and I took my time, getting up late. I'd finished my first week of in-hospital chemotherapy the previous week, and as I sat with a warm cup of tea, a childhood memory came to mind.

I was nine years old, and we were living in Colombia. Friday night had brought everybody out in the streets. Some children played soccer, while parents listened to tango tunes and melancholic ballads from their small transistor radios. Some of the teenagers had been talking about marathon running, and tonight seemed to be a good night for emulating some of the great distance runners. Excitement erupted when some of the adults decided to challenge their younger sons. The race would involve running around the block twenty-six times, and the dads were sure they would show their sons who was better. I got caught up in the excitement and wanted to run too, but I was younger and smaller than they were. Despite a lot of resistance because of my age, I was allowed to run with the pack but not without many words of caution from the mothers: "Take a break if you need to"; "Drink plenty of water"; "You can quit if you want to."

My first "mile" felt fast as I tried to keep up with everybody. I could already tell I was not going to win the race, as my legs felt heavy and lacked power. Perhaps I could finish near the top. Halfway through, some people started to drop out of the race. My childish dream of doing the marathon gradually started to take on a more realistic picture as my legs started to get tired. I was eventually able to find my breathing, and I figured if I could keep that slow, steady pace, I would probably finish the race. That was an accomplishment that some already had let go. The last five laps got easier for me as the crowd began to cheer me on. I was the only nine-year-old still running laps. Actually, I was the only one still running at that point, as the other competitors had already finished the race, an event won neither by dads nor teenagers but by a twenty-year-old already attending the university.

As I crossed the line, I felt very proud of myself: I'd run around the block twenty-six times without taking a break or a sip of water. More important, I finished the race, and I could tell that this American boy had gained respect among the elders. The image that became ingrained in my memory that night was the comfortable pace that I found halfway through the race while I was determined and focused to cross the finish line. It was an image where I knew people were outside, radios were playing, and cars were going by, yet for me, there was complete silence, except for the sound of my even-paced breathing and footsteps on the road.

I have endured tough competitions at other times in my life. Roller hockey tournaments in high school and soccer games in college were physically demanding. More enduring were final exams in college and medical school—staying up late at night and cutting my sleep short, drinking coffee by the hour, trying to memorize the last fact or squeeze in one more paragraph in that term paper, living life literally by the hour because it seemed like every day should be twenty-five hours long instead. Yet these events seemed short and perhaps relatively easy compared to what I had now embarked.

If there was a race that I was going to run and cross the finish line, this was it! Twelve weeks of chemotherapy during the summer of 1985—a long, mundane, boring run that had only one purpose to it: to save my life. In my mind, I had done this race before. I simply had to pace myself for twelve weeks of chemotherapy, which would take the whole summer, and then have one more surgery in September. There was a fixed amount of time to accomplish this. There was a beginning and an end. This was just like running around the block twenty-six times, not one block more or one less.

The intellectually challenging part of this chemotherapy was trying to figure out what "pacing myself" would entail. I began by becoming completely focused on myself. Whatever my body told me to do, I did. Prior to my diagnosis, I had been running three to four times a week, averaging about twelve to fifteen miles a week. I was able to run through the month of June and part of July but had to give it up as I gradually became weak and lost strength in my legs. Not only did my legs become weak, but also my breathing became more labored, even during short runs. Running gave way to walking, and eventually, I became completely sedentary by September. I was disappointed to give up exercising, but I knew the war had not been lost.

Nutrition became the most important element during the summer, as I gradually lost weight from not eating during the weeks that I was hospitalized for chemotherapy and from having a suboptimal appetite over the two weeks before the next hospitalization. Although I had become mad at God during this period, I believe God cared for me and touched me through other people's help—God's messengers, if you will. And so it was that Anne met an oncology nurse that summer.

Anne had finished her second year of law school and was doing a summer internship at a prosecutor's office in Port Huron, Michigan. The attorney she worked for knew a friend who was an oncology nurse who worked across the lake in Canada, and she helped Anne by talking to her about chemotherapy and its untoward side effects. The oncology nurse also was the one who passed on tips on how to help me with my nutrition while I went through chemotherapy.

At the oncology's nurse suggestion, I began to eat basic foods to help my nutritional status. For breakfast, I had cream of wheat that was iron-fortified, apple juice, oatmeal toast, and vitamins. For lunch, I tried to eat soups and meat sandwiches. I had a protein-fortified milkshake twice a day. For dinner, I frequently had scrambled eggs and toast, brown rice, and apple juice. I was fortunate that my hemoglobin never dropped below nine, and my white-blood-cell count never dropped below two thousand. The risks of infection would increase when the white-blood-cell count dropped below 1,500.

The apple juice was very soothing to my mouth. As my white-blood-cell count dropped from each round of chemotherapy, I began to develop ulcers in my mouth along the gums, tongue, and inner cheeks. I also drank a lot of apple juice to keep hydrated and flush out the chemotherapy.

I did see my weight drop from 186 pounds before diagnosis to about 140 pounds after the last surgery. But I truly believe that the little I was able to eat from the above diet kept me from getting major complications.

Another element in maintaining a good pace was getting as much rest as possible. My sleep cycle was always thrown off during the weeks that I was hospitalized for chemotherapy. I received Ativan at high doses, a drug to help the nausea and vomiting, but it was also a sedative and an amnesiac. I found myself sleeping at different times of the day and then being fully awake at night. I also received Thorazine, which is an antipsychotic, because it also had antinausea properties. The hospitalization would last five days, Monday through Friday. After the hospital discharge, it would usually take me two to maybe three days to get adjusted with my sleep cycles again. It felt good to get almost two weeks of good sleep before the next hospitalization. I napped often and had an average of about ten to twelve hours of sleep at night. (Medicines today for fighting nausea and vomiting with chemotherapy are better and have fewer side effects.)

Because I became so focused on myself, eating at the right times with the right foods and sleeping as often as my body felt like doing, I gradually detached myself from my friends. I felt like I had enough support from Anne. Interestingly enough, taking care of my brother Bob and my dad gave me an additional purpose that summer. While they both worked during the day, I cooked meals, did the grocery shopping, did the laundry, and kept the place clean. I think the German in me helped me through this phase. I simply had to put my head down and plow through.

I also tried to study for the National Boards of Medical Examiners part one. During those days, medical students typically took this test after their second year of medical school. I had a difficult time studying for this test, as my mind was always pretty foggy. It was difficult to concentrate and to focus. As a consequence, I did not pass the test that September but retook it the next year and did well.

Despite all the adversity, I had my moments of laughter. I will never forget the third weekend after I started chemotherapy. Anne and I had decided to go to Wisconsin for a weekend trip. We found a place on Lake Geneva and met the owner, a nice lady in her sixties. I knew my hair was getting close to coming off—it had been three weeks since I had started chemotherapy—but it happened that Saturday morning, and most of my hair was on the pillow when I woke up. After taking a shower and pulling the rest of my hair off, we checked out of the room. Anne and I could not stop laughing as we were checking out because I was bald, and I had left all my hair in the wastebasket.

I also remember the weekend when I went to visit Anne in Port Huron, Michigan. She was staying at her boss's lake house for the weekend, and there were two cats at the house. I did not care for cats, particularly, so we opted to leave them outside the bedroom. After much whining from one of the cats, this obnoxious feline walked out of the house and climbed on the roof. She showed up at our window and began to whine from there. She was persistent and would not take no for an answer.

Sometimes with cancer, we develop a bizarre sense of humor. It must be a coping mechanism. Anyway, one of my favorite stories happened during my last round of chemotherapy. The veins in my arms were frail and scarred from the chemotherapy. It was very difficult to get an IV in my veins or, much worse, to make it last more than a day. A nurse with an Eastern European accent was taking care of me, and she became very frustrated when my IV pump kept going off when I would throw up—I couldn't help bending my arms when I threw up. On one of her visits, she finally said, "If you're going to throw up, you must throw up with your arm straight." Go ahead; you try it!

These stories may not seem very funny, but at the time, with my mind so foggy, weird things like these seemed pretty hilarious.

I had my last surgery at the end of September 1985. I still had some tumor in my retroperitoneum, and the pathology report showed teratomas (benign residual tumors). I was considered a partial responder to chemotherapy but was cured of the disease after the surgery. It was hard to recover from this last surgery. I was very weak and had dropped a lot of weight. After being discharged from

Indiana University, I went to Kalamazoo, Michigan, to recover at Anne's parents' house. Unfortunately, I started throwing up twenty-four hours later, and within two days, I became very dehydrated. I was readmitted at one of our local hospitals in Kalamazoo for vomiting and dehydration. I had what is termed an *adynamic ileus*, where basically my bowels had gone to sleep, and it would take some time for them to wake up and start working again. The combined hospitalization, between both hospitals, lasted fifteen days. My intestines simply took too long to get back to work, and I was not able to eat for long time.

Two events during the readmission and second hospitalization made me feel touched by God. The first one was related to a nurse on the night shift, who probably saw me as a frail, skinny, and bald-headed cancer patient whose body was beaten down and worn out. After she took vital signs on all her patients at the beginning of her 7:00 p.m. shift, she would come in to give me a back rub, which felt very peaceful. My muscles were very tense, and I could tell I had experienced severe physical stress after throwing up for two days straight, prior to readmission, and this was only nine days after I'd had major abdominal surgery. Her touch was warm and soothing. I felt God trying to heal me through her hands, trying to let me know that I was going to be OK and would recover eventually. Time was on my side, and I just needed to find some peace.

The second event occurred the morning that Rock Hudson passed away. I had not eaten in almost two weeks and had a nasogastric tube in my nose that went down to my stomach, pulling up all those juices and acid from my stomach since my bowels were asleep. I was feeling pretty weak at the time as I watched the news on TV, and I went into a semiawake, dreamlike state. I felt like my body rose to the ceiling, and I could actually see myself in bed, watching the TV. It was a very peaceful and loving state, and I was empathizing with Rock Hudson as they discussed his death. I felt like I was asked if I wanted to die and stay in that state or if I wanted to go back. My immediate thought was of Anne and that we had gotten engaged the previous Christmas. I decided I did not want to leave Anne alone, and I made the conscious decision to return to my body; to persevere, even though I was exhausted. Later that day, I developed bowel sounds that indicated my bowels had started to move, so I asked to have my NG tube removed and began to take clear liquids later that night. Sitting up in bed led to walking out in the hallways as I started moving forward with my recovery.

The recovery took a few more days before I was able to eat solids, enough to be discharged from the hospital. Seeing light on the horizon helped me acknowledge how helpful Anne had been to me. Throughout the entire summer and now, we talked often with words of encouragement and used humor on a regular basis to help us deal with the anxiety and stress. I have always admired her sports-like competitive nature and her sense to not be defeated.

As I left the hospital and went to Anne's parents' home to recover, the reality of weighing 140 pounds—really skinny—began to sink in. I was weak; walking even one block was exhausting. I wanted to get back to the basics of being normal, to enjoy everyday living—eating, walking, and sleeping. I napped often, sometimes twice a day. The cool air of October and the changing of the leaves made me feel peaceful in my transition to a new life. At least for that month of October, I didn't have to worry about chemotherapy, feeling nauseated, my weak veins, getting IVs started, blood draws, surgeries, or any other uncertainty. All the noise was behind me, and I felt that I could stroll down the sidewalk, contemplating the yellow, orange, and red leaves on the trees, bundled up with two sweaters, winter coat, hat, and winter gloves in fifty-degree weather (not that cold by Michigan standards), and feel peaceful that nobody could touch me.

The following month, Dad and I took a trip to the Bahamas. I had been dreaming about having a Heineken beer out on the beach as a way to celebrate my victory. With the temperature in the eighties and the sun on my back, I stared at the ocean and the blue sky for the first time in many months and felt alive. As I gave thanks to God, I was willing to acknowledge that God had helped me through all of this, but I still felt that our relationship was strained. I did not feel that connection with God as I had in the past. I wondered why God had put me through this hardship. I had lost my trust in God, and my faith in God had diminished. I even questioned whether God could or would hear my prayers.

I was willing, however, to acknowledge that God had used messengers to help me along the way. My medical school classmates were there to help me with school and companionship. There were many nights when one or more of them spent time with me while I got my chemotherapy. The oncology nurse was like an angel to Anne while she worked in Port Huron, and her advice on nutrition was invaluable. Anne's parents stood by me, particularly toward the end of my treatments, when we had to make the decision for readmission in September and then with my recovery during October. Bless Anne's brother, Rob, for cleaning up all the vomit I had during those forty-eight hours prior to readmission. Anne's friend Sharon was a constant support to both of us. The Regos family in Chicago always had a motherly way of caring for both Anne and me, whether it was through meals or companionship. My dad and my brother Bob gave me a sense of purpose, and we always found ways to have a laugh. Deep down, I felt love from all and felt hope that I could recover with their help. This gave me insight that our relationship with God is not just one-dimensional, where I am praying to God; in fact, God works through us all so that we can help each other. God loves to gaze at us when we can help each other out.

# Chapter 4

# Cancer Relapses

*November 2001*

Anne and I got married in 1986, and we lived in Illinois while I finished medical school and pediatric residency training. We moved to Kalamazoo, Michigan, and had our two children. I was enjoying practicing pediatric care and marveled at how the kids were growing up. Tim had started playing soccer, and Patty, as a two-year-old, had exploded with her vocabulary, reading everything and entertaining us with her sense of humor. It was 1998 when I found out I was having a relapse with my testicular cancer.

We used to do hospital rounds at both the nursery and the pediatric hospital floor at both local hospitals, and it was my turn that week to do hospital rounds for the group. It was a busy day when I got scheduled for additional tests. I got up at five o'clock in the morning so that I could start my hospital rounds at one hospital, travel to the second hospital to get my tests done, and finally be back to the office by two o'clock in the afternoon to see patients. The waiting room in the lab at the second hospital was already full by eight in the morning, and I second-guessed myself for having seen patients at the first hospital, rather than having had my blood drawn at six o'clock in the morning, when the waiting room would have been practically empty. I was supposed to have a CT scan at nine, and I felt that I was cutting it close with my time schedule.

Once I got done with the CT scans, I needed to do hospital rounds at the second hospital, take a quick lunch, and then have an ultrasound of my lone testicle at one that afternoon. If all went well, I could make it back to the office by two and then see patients until five.

I guess you could say I was busy that day. I could feel the adrenaline pumping through my system. My hands felt clammy, and my body felt tight. I checked my pulse, and my heart rate was about ninety beats per minute, where it usually would be in the fifties by late evening. My legs felt restless, and I wanted to fidget in my chair, but I had learned to appear calm and stay still. I picked up a magazine and looked at my watch; it seemed like a lot of time had passed, but it was only 8:05 a.m.

Out of a group of about twenty people waiting to get their tests done, only one had gone through in the past five minutes. Many thoughts raced through my mind as I tried to remain in control of my schedule. I thought about the babies in the nurseries, and I was glad that they were stable. The kids on the pediatric floors needed a couple of days of treatment, and they would then be ready to go home.

I wondered why people were not going through the line any faster. Were the techs having a hard time drawing blood today? I thought about walking up to the secretary and explaining to her that I was a physician and that I had a busy schedule that day. She probably would not mind if I wanted to cut in line and be the next person to get my blood drawn. Maybe I would have to explain myself to the other patients and ask them to excuse me for cutting in. Perhaps they would understand as well.

It seemed like all I had to do was work up the guts to do this, and then I would be on my way. As I scanned the room and tried to feel how everybody would react, I realized that there was one lady who would probably mind. She looked tired and frustrated. Her shoulders drooped, and she stared at the floor. Maybe she was upset at her illness or perhaps at her doctor. She would probably yell at me, "I am a patient too, and nothing makes you more special than me." I then realized that perhaps everybody in the room would feel the same way, although they might not show it.

As my disposition began to change, I began to blend in with everybody in the room. I had a disease, just like they did. I was a patient with a job, family, some friends, perhaps a house and a car, and, yes, a disease. I began to appreciate that I had no right to jump in ahead of them. I guess, after all these years of being cancer-free, I was still a patient. That was my identity. I was a cancer patient with a likely relapse.

As I sat in the room and stared at the beige walls, the pictures of nature, and the people walking by the lab, I realized that I needed to relax. I took a deep breath and exhaled it slowly. Another deep breath and another slow exhale. My pulse began to slow down, and my muscles loosened up. Who would have thought that after being cancer-free for thirteen years that I would be dealing with a cancer relapse?

As I became more relaxed in the waiting room, I developed a sense of weightlessness in my body. I closed my eyes and felt like I was starting to float in the room. The anxiety of meeting all these deadlines disappeared. A sense of confidence settled in that I would be able to get everything done that day. I simply had to "float" through the day. I visualized myself floating through the hospital floors, moving with uncanny speed and with effortless maneuvering around the corners. My decision-making was going to be simple and quick.

The results of the CT scans later that day confirmed that I was having a cancer relapse. There were four masses in my retroperitoneum, the back portion of my abdomen area, one of them tightly involved with my right kidney and its blood vessels. I discussed my results with Dr. Einhorn at Indiana University, and we talked about options. Chemotherapy was not as effective as surgery, so I opted for the latter.

By March 1999, I was ready for surgery. My emotions were more in control, compared to the scare that I had had in 1990. I was a third-year resident at the time, and one of my tumor markers, the b-HCG, was elevated. Over a forty-eight-hour period, I had my blood drawn three times and had one pregnancy test done—I always had wanted to do this. The pregnancy test is based on the hormone b-HCG, and one of my tumors had made this. After much anxiety and worry over those forty-eight hours, my repeat tests came back normal—and I was not pregnant!

This time around, I felt more in control. I had seen the emotional relapse beast once already, and I did not need to give it any more importance or attention than it needed to have. I was ready to get back into fighting form, as I had in 1985. I was ready to win again. This time around, I had two more reasons to fight: our two children, six-year-old Tim and two-year-old Patty. I was determined not to leave Anne alone with two children. It is very hard, although not impossible, to raise children as a single parent. I felt that Anne could do a good job by herself, but I also felt a strong sense of responsibility to help Anne out.

As we drove to Indianapolis, I became very focused on how my recovery was going to go. I could visualize waking up from anesthesia, having all those tubes and IVs sticking out of me, dealing with the pain from my abdominal incision, and doing laps down the corridor floor and around the nurses' station to get my bowels working. I could see myself drinking liquids and hopefully not getting sick with vomiting.

As I went through the preanesthesia routine, I began to get a little nervous. My hands felt cold and clammy as I placed my blue booties on my feet and my surgical cap on my head. I zoned out as I heard conversations between my dad; Dad's wife, Ellen; and Anne. My mind became blank, not knowing what to think, as mental tiredness sank in. The surroundings engulfed me—the antiseptic smell permeated the waiting room; the nurse's footsteps provided a rhythm of comfort; the energy from the ceiling fluorescent lights gave life to my heart. As I sat in the brown reclining chair, wearing nothing but a blue gown, blue booties, and surgical cap, I dropped into limbo and rested for a while.

When the surgical nurse came back to take me to the operating room, I offered to walk rather than go in a wheelchair. Feeling incapacitated was not an option; being prepared for battle and wanting to feel self-confident was at the forefront of my fighting spirit. I wanted to show determination and a strong attitude. Yellow ceramic tile lined the halls, the lighting was dim, and the floor was the all-too-familiar brown tile. I paused at the entrance of the operating room and looked at the bed with white sheets and beige blanket. My eyes then glanced at the nurses doing their instrument counts and getting ready for surgery. The anesthesiologist was checking the gases while he wrote on his clipboard.

All of sudden, I couldn't move. I continued to stand by the entrance and felt a desire to run away. I wasn't sure where I was going to go, but I was not going to back to the waiting room. I needed to go somewhere where nobody could catch me. I could see myself running down the hall as my gown lifted up, making me look like Batman. The nurse and orderly would run behind me yelling, "Stop that patient! He has escaped the surgery room!" But it seemed ridiculous for a physician to be running away from surgery. After all, I had gotten used to being in control of my emotions, despite all the life-or-death situations in which I had been involved, taking care of pediatric patients.

This whole scenario, which probably took only a few seconds, came to a halt as I saw the nurses and anesthesiologist staring at me after they greeted me with a warm welcome. I returned a nervous smile and proceeded to lie on the bed. A little sedation helped me relax, and soon after, I was asleep.

Surgery went well—better than I had expected. I had prayed

to God to help the surgeon save my right kidney and felt that my prayers had been answered, as he was able to remove the tumor that was embedded with the vein to that right kidney. The other three masses were removed easily, and the entire surgery lasted only five hours. I woke up from anesthesia more easily, as compared to 1985, and was not surprised by all the invasive tubes and monitors. After a six-day hospital stay, I was released and chose to stay at the hotel across the street, just in case I started to throw up like I did in September 1985. Hopefully, if I had a restful and uneventful night, we could drive back to Michigan, and I would be on my way to full recovery.

Unfortunately, I woke up in the middle of the night and began to throw up. Within a couple of hours of throwing up a few times, we decided to go back to the emergency room and get readmitted. I had to have another NG tube passed down my nose and throat to my stomach, which would help my stomach settle down. It turned out be a long night in the emergency room without getting any sleep.

Once admitted to the hospital later in the morning and not long after I settled into the same room from which I had been discharged the previous day, the morning shift came in, and the sun began to rise. It had been a long night from not having any sleep, and I felt exhausted. When my daytime nurse came in to change my bed sheets, I moved to the sofa and stared into space. My shoulders felt heavy, and my heart was depressed. After days of doing laps on the hospital floor to help my bowels move, I felt defeated. X-rays of my abdomen showed that my bowels had gone back to sleep. I was back to square one—and who knew how long I would remain in the hospital with that NG tube sticking out of my nose? My eyes got watery, and my throat cramped up. It didn't seem fair to have this much suffering. I thought I could make myself better. I followed all the instructions for recovery, and I actually felt like a pro, as I had already done this.

I pitied myself like I never had before. I was pathetic. It didn't matter that the sunlight pierced the room; my heart was filled with darkness. It was empty and devoid of love and comfort. I wanted to simply burst out in a big cry, but I couldn't. There was a nurse in the room, and I was not going to let her see me cry. As I gazed out the door, I had this feeling that my grandma Murphy was with me. It was odd because I had not been thinking about her. In pure Grandma Murphy form, she lifted her index finger at me and told me to snap out of it. "Quit feeling sorry for yourself. You are going to be fine, and you will walk away from this hospital. You simply need to be patient." These words, of course, were my interpretation of the feeling that I had in a split second, but it was powerful and everlasting. I hung on to those words for the rest of the hospitalization.

I wiped my tears and decided to change my attitude. Although the days became boring and long as I shifted from lying in bed, to watching TV, to sleeping and napping, I finally felt a peace that told me I was going to recover. I simply needed to be patient.

It was the beginning of spring when I came home. The cold air chilled my bones as I went out for my first walk. The trees had no leaves, but the sun was bright, casting tree shadows over the streets as they reflected the scars in my soul. Not only was I physically tired and weak after losing twenty pounds, but I also felt emotionally and spiritually depleted. If there was any consolation, I had made it through so that I could be with my family again. I felt different with my inner self this time around. Whereas in 1985, I'd felt that all recovery was based on my own will, I felt this time that I had needed some extra help at the hospital. It was Grandma Murphy who came to the rescue and gave me some peace. It was Anne's patience, perseverance, and hard work that helped me with the daily challenges. I gradually began to walk, going from one block to two blocks to eventually a mile. And as I progressed from walking, I began to run again. Two months later, I was back to work and taking care of kids.

As the summer-morning breeze swept through the flowers in

our backyard, and the robins sang their wake-up calls, a new era had started for me. In church that Sunday morning, I thanked God for letting me get back to my life and to be with my family. I felt proud that I had done a good job with my recovery. It seemed like it was a little bit of God's will and big chunk of my will. I felt in control again with my health, my work, and my exercising and eating. The problem was that I felt restless in my heart, as if God was tugging at me, and I did not want to comply.

By August of that year, I began to feel the wear of not being able to sleep well through the night. I thought my sleep patterns would get back to normal after they had been disrupted in the spring, but this carried through the summer, and now I was feeling tired. I was restless at night and woke up many times. My body felt tight and anxious. I followed Anne's recommendation to get a body massage one day. It was a wonderful experience. My body felt so relaxed; I felt I could have fallen asleep right after the massage. I opted to get another massage a few weeks later, but I did not experience the same relaxation. Although my muscles felt light, I felt a void in my heart. I was hungry for more, but I wasn't sure what. I continued to think that perhaps my restlessness was still part of my recovery from surgery and from the emotional upheaval of dealing with cancer again. But I got worse with my compulsiveness at home and at work. I got irritated easily and did not tolerate poor performance anywhere. My restless nights continued without relief.

As the leaves began to change colors and the air became crisp and cool, I entered a new phase in my life. Anne encouraged me to talk with our friend Pauline, a Christian Scientist and very devout in prayer. I learned that I was hanging onto life too tightly. I was not letting God take care of me. This was such a revelation that evening that after talking with Pauline for ninety minutes, I felt like a ton of bricks had been lifted off my shoulders. That night, I prayed to God to help me with my struggles. The next morning, after I dropped my son off at kindergarten, I walked into church to pray. There had been only a handful of times in my life when

I had gone into church to pray when it was not Sunday, but it felt right to do so this time. I wanted to improve my relationship with God and to better understand myself spiritually. I wanted to talk to God on a more regular basis. I needed to learn to let go and let God take care of me.

# Chapter 5

# Daily Prayer

*December 2001*

T his chapter has been difficult to prepare. I have spent a fair amount of time thinking about it and about what I would like to say. My challenge lies in that I can hardly consider myself an expert in prayer, yet I feel that this chapter is of paramount importance to the message I am trying to convey.

As I walk through the spirituality and Christianity aisles at the bookstore, I can easily find numerous books on prayer. It is interesting that many people have felt compelled to write about prayer. There is that mystical part of us that links us to God or another supreme being, and we can communicate with each other through prayer.

The knowledge I have gained on prayer comes from a handful of books, from talks with parish priests, and from my daily prayer. I can tell, however, from the books I have read that there are people, either alive or deceased, who have experienced prayer better than I have. I consider myself still a rookie with much more to learn, if God is willing. In fact, I would say that people I've met at my office, either coworkers or parents, are just as deep or deeper in prayer than what I am capable of doing at this time. I have come to appreciate that praying is an art that transfigures itself with time; it is God-driven, and it grows and becomes more powerful in time with God's love. As a vehicle of communication, it needs to be nurtured and practiced on a regular basis, or it will become rustic and awkward. In the same way that I experience awkwardness when I haven't ridden a bicycle, juggled a soccer ball, or spoken a foreign language in a while, prayer also can become awkward if I don't practice regularly. As a consequence, it becomes one-sided, where I ask God for favors, but I don't hear God in my heart—a language that is unspoken.

When my friend Pauline made the comment that I was hanging on to life too hard and was not letting God live through me, I felt compelled to go to church on weekdays and pray to God. I already got a special feeling when I went to church on Sundays. As soon as the doors would close behind me, I would feel quietness in my heart. All the activity and commotion from the day would disappear. A sense of respect and humbleness took over as I walked down the aisle toward my pew. But going to church during the week seemed odd and different, out of the ordinary, somewhat awkward.

I started to go to church in the mornings after dropping Tim at school. Initially, I found myself able to pray for only about five minutes. I would start my praying, which was what I typically did on Sundays before mass, consisting of thanking God for recent positive experiences, asking God for forgiveness of my faults, and asking for help in areas of need. On Sundays, I tried to get in the prayer of Saint Francis before or after Communion, so I decided to pray with this style on weekdays as well.

Saint Francis was born in 1118 in Assisi, Italy.[4] The son of a wealthy family, he was moved in his late teens to turn down his family business and welfare to help the poor. His personal changes were drastic, and initially, his community saw him as irrational; he was once seen walking nude in his village, as he did not want to wear the clothing that associated him with wealth. He later settled for a simple brown robe. He represented a force in action that seemed contrary to the Catholic Church at the time. His life was one of simplicity and addressed the basics of life. With time, the people in his community—and later on, the church—came to appreciate him for all the good services he provided to people. He wrote many prayers, but he seems to be better known for his Prayer of Saint Francis, although there is some question whether he wrote it himself:

Lord, make an instrument of your peace,
Where there is hatred,
Let me sow love;
Where there is injury, pardon;
Where there is doubt, faith;
Where there is despair, hope;
Where there is darkness, light;
And where there is sadness, joy.
O Divine Master, grant that I may not
So much seek to be consoled as to console;
To be understood as to understand;
To be loved as to love.
For it is giving that we receive,
It is in pardoning that we are pardoned,
And it is dying
That we are born to eternal life.

I learned about Saint Francis of Assisi when I was in high school in Cali, Colombia. I attended a Catholic school of Franciscan denomination. Every morning, prior to the start of classes, we would gather on the large patio in the middle of the school and pray the Prayer of Saint Francis. I learned the prayer in Spanish, and to this day, I still pray it in Spanish, as it seems to flow more naturally for me. Over the years, however, the prayer became mechanical for me. I mostly prayed it in my head, as I would try to accentuate every word in my mind, but I seemed to lack fervor in my heart.

It was September 1999 when I began to go to church on

weekday mornings, averaging about two to three mornings per week. I couldn't seem to get past five minutes in prayer before my mind would wander. I also wondered what all the people in church were praying about at 7:30 in the morning. Not only was walking into church on weekdays a change and a discovery for me, but it was a revelation to find that I was not the only one praying in the morning. There were typically twenty to thirty people in the age range of fifties to seventies. I became friends with a couple of guys who seemed to be in their sixties. We would acknowledge each other's presence with a head nod or a smile as we sat in the back of the church. I later learned that they were praying the rosary before eight o'clock mass.

As I became more comfortable and relaxed with going to church in the mornings, I began to lengthen my prayers to ten minutes and gradually to fifteen minutes. I would essentially say the same prayers but more slowly so that I could feel the words better. This became very pleasant and soothing to my soul. My body and mind would feel relaxed, and I did not feel rushed to get to work. Whenever I did not have a meeting or paperwork to take care of, I would try to make it to church that morning. I looked forward to it so much that I tried to increase my attendance to four, sometimes five, mornings a week.

This time of praying became essential to my well-being, as my pediatric group had asked me to become the head of the department. By going to church, I could relieve the stress created by all the administrative challenges that went along with being the person in charge. This was a new situation for me, and I welcomed the challenge. In my religious naiveté, I thought I could handle two opposing forces and reconcile their opposing energies: trying to handle a busy work life with a more relaxed, prayerful life. As I looked back a year after stepping down, as my turn was over, I realized that I did not have the spiritual maturity to handle such a position. I frequently let the frustrations and workload disrupt the peacefulness that I was trying to attain with my daily morning prayer.

In fact, after a couple of months of doing my daily morning prayer, I began to wonder if I was praying properly because I was disturbed frequently during the day. I didn't necessarily show it on the outside, but inside, I would feel restless, frustrated, and not peaceful.

I would say that some good came from this Prayer of Saint Francis, as I tried to give myself completely to God and take care of the young patients. When it came to administrative work, however, I seemed to experience two different worlds. I thought my ideas and suggestions were coming from my heart and soul, but as I look back, I can tell that was not the case. My mind and will were actively at work. Frequently, what my mind and will wanted was not necessarily what was right in my heart and soul, and I began to have a greater appreciation of that.

I gradually lost perspective on what was considered important in life and what was not. I got caught up in material matters that seemed important in everyday life but had no bearing on my spiritual development. In addition, pride made me feel that I was capable of handling the administrative responsibilities. Pride, in fact, made me feel that I was the cause of my success. I was taking good care of children, and I was heading my department. On the outside, it seemed like I was doing a good job with both activities.

Within a year, I found myself far away from the shore. The revelation I had experienced in September 1999, when I wanted to start daily prayer, was gone. It was easy to repress my feelings of restlessness and continue to work on a daily basis on administrative issues that made the practice successful. I continued to go to church in the mornings, but I did not know how to get closer to God. I couldn't see the path, and it was easy just to continue in the dark, although I had no idea that I *was* in the dark.

I felt that my praying had hit a stumbling block, so I opted to speak to one of our parish priests. I mentioned how my prayer went every morning when I came to church. I was methodical, and I almost never deviated from the same prayers from day to day. I also said these prayers in the same order, every day. Yet I had lost that feeling of peacefulness and relaxation.

The priest suggested that I read a book titled *The Soul of the Apostolate* by Dom Jean Baptiste Cheataurd.[5] Fr. Jean Baptiste was a brilliant and ardent Cistercian abbot from France, born in 1858. He was instrumental in resurrecting and keeping alive the Cistercian order. At a time when the Catholic Church was fighting political battles and was dealing with decreased faith in its community, the church opted to build large churches, hold conventions, and build more schools to influence the people to come back to the church. Fr. Jean Baptiste chose, instead, to resurrect the development of the interior life as the means to rebuild the church.

In his book, Fr. Jean Baptiste explains the significance of the interior life and how it relates to the active life. The latter is everything that surrounds us, the physical world, and how we, as the human race, maintain this physical world. For example, the active life would be the time we spend on a project and the effort we spend to see it bear its fruits. Another example would be our participation in a group that wants to do some kind of charity. And still one more example: the managing of our finances to make sure we have enough money for house payments and groceries.

The interior life, however, is the soul's state of activity that strives to follow the teachings of the gospel and follow the examples of Jesus and God. At the same time, the interior life attempts to fight against the soul's natural inclination to follow its own will. Interestingly enough, although the active life and interior life are two different entities, they are dependent on each other. Too much of the active life leads to very little of the interior life, and vice versa. The ideal life finds the balance between these two lives. For example, we need the active life because good deeds, by the grace of God, can increase the supernatural in our interior life. By the same token, improvements in our interior life can lead, by the grace of God, to better handling of the challenges in the active life. Eventually, the state of complete happiness comes from the union of our souls and interior lives with

God, of our wills with that of God's. This achievement is difficult to attain here on earth because we struggle to balance the active life and the interior life.

It took me about one year to finish Fr. Jean Baptiste's book. I am a slow reader, but this book was so deep in matters of the interior life that I could read only two to three pages at a time. I incorporated reading this book into my morning prayer, which then led me to meditate on what Fr. Jean Baptiste said. Thanks to the priest, I began what is called *meditative prayer*. I have now reread this book a second time and have found that I am still learning about the interior life.

In meditative prayer, you can think, ponder, feel, suffer, or rejoice on an aspect of God, Jesus, or his life. Here, you are not necessarily asking God for a favor or thanking him for a good deed. You may read from a book, which then prompts you to think or feel deeply about God and God's love, and then see how it relates to your life.

For me, it was an opportunity to experience Jesus' feeling of humility and meekness when Mary and Joseph found him at the temple or, at other times, to feel his suffering when he was on the cross. I must admit that I am not sure I could ever feel what he felt, as I have never been crucified, but perhaps I've had some taste of it. With my big surgeries in Indianapolis, I usually had IV sticks and needles, an NG tube through my nose and down my throat, a Foley catheter, an arterial line from my wrist, an incision wound up and down my abdomen, and the body discomfort that comes from not being able to eat or sleep soundly during those early days of post-op recovery. All these feelings have given me an appreciation for what Jesus went through. And to think that he did that for us. His sacrifice and Resurrection gave us hope that our souls could be saved. The death of his body and the Resurrection of his body and soul gives us hope that our bodies and souls also will rise to be near God. Being with God must be wonderful! I can only imagine how wonderful this must be because I have had glimpses of feeling God's peacefulness and love by letting God flow through me completely. I emphasize *glimpses* because it has been very difficult for me to feel God's love and peacefulness all the time. There is too much distraction and there are too many temptations that make it hard for me to be one with God.

I used to think that the purpose in life was to become a better person. After my first relapse with cancer and finding regular prayer, I changed my view: the purpose in life was to master the external world so that I could develop my soul and make it a fitting home for God to dwell in. I felt that the mastering of my active life could not come from my intellect but from my interior life. Later, I found myself changing this view again (as I will describe later).

With meditative prayer occurring on a regular basis and not just mental prayer, as I had done initially, I found myself enjoying church again. I could sense that I was drawing closer to God during these times of prayer. But as I drew closer to God and my prayer lengthened to about twenty to twenty-five minutes, my meditation seemed to enter a new phase. My mind began to wander frequently.

An example of a morning prayer went like this: I walked into church one morning and began with a few prayers. I pondered on Jesus's ability to be understanding and how I could improve my ability to understand. I reflected on the Prayer of Saint Francis, which then led me to think about how I could be more understanding with my two-year-old daughter as she struggled with her bedtime routine. Pretty soon, my mind left prayer, and I was somewhere else. I continued to think about her getting out of bed every night, several times a night. Maybe she was scared of the dark. I then wondered if I had been too harsh with her the night before and then felt a little guilty. Perhaps developmentally, she was not ready to have all the lights turned off yet. Maybe I needed to take that course in developmental pediatrics that was coming up soon so I could be more understanding of her. I wondered how much that course would cost and whether I had enough money in my continuing medical education account to attend that course. I thought I needed to give our office manager a call to find out if I had enough money.

And just like that, I was out on left field with my praying, thinking about matters that perhaps were important in the active life but had nothing to do with my interior life. A few minutes went by before I caught myself being off course, and I then had to refocus. Following Dom Jean Baptiste's advice, I would read again some material to help me focus and get back to prayer. He does caution us, however, not to rely much on reading when these problems occur because this is the easy way out. He would rather see us place ourselves in God's hands and contemplate God's love. This last concept was certainly foreign in my heart.

I stayed with mental and meditative prayer for a while, not able to totally understand how to rest in God's hands, letting God take the lead in prayer. In fact, I stayed in this state of prayer until I had my second cancer relapse. Oddly enough, one day when I was at church in one of my morning prayers, I received a split-second image or vision that my cancer was going to come back, and I saw my left hip and left leg highlighted, but I would recover after that relapse. I wasn't sure why the left hip and leg were highlighted and wondered if I would have to have those areas amputated, but I felt that I could do that, if that was what God wanted me to do. I wondered if I was being insecure and had made this up. Not wanting to dwell on it, I put it in the back of my head and continued with my daily routines in prayer and work.

# Chapter 6

# Contemplative Prayer

*January 2002*

The year 1999, after my first cancer relapse, was one of tremendous spiritual growth. I found myself praying several times a week and usually left church in a peaceful state. I began to feel that I wanted to be with God all the time. I thought about God often throughout the day and made frequent ejaculatory prayers. These prayers were usually short one-liners, where I acknowledged God's presence and asked for a favor or expressed gratitude. I might, for example, feel God's presence and ask for God's help as I was trying to clean a child's ear. The risky process entailed cleaning wax out of the ear with a metal curette, while sometimes the child struggled because he or she was held down on the examining table. I needed to be careful not to get too close to the eardrum while still getting the wax out.

The closer I felt to God, the more difficult it became to be here on earth. I began to think and feel that life on earth was too complicated and fast-paced. I struggled many times a day with matters that didn't seem to have a major consequence spiritually.

Perhaps they were important in the function of the external world or active life, but they frequently distracted me from pursuing the development of my interior life. Leaving church in the morning was becoming a struggle. Did I really have to go to work? Why couldn't I just stay in church and feel God's presence?

I felt passive-aggressive at work and at home. Sometimes, I would get involved with a task to be helpful but would let go of it easily if I came across the smallest obstacle. However, I did not let go of my responsibilities and wanted to make sure I did my job.

The harder I pressed to carry on with the active life and interior life at the same time, the wider the sea seemed to split apart. These two lives did not mix well, and I did not have enough spiritual maturity to reconcile their differences.

Pride was certainly becoming the biggest obstacle to my interior-life development. Although I had started to believe and felt better that God was with me and helped me a lot, I still felt that many of my accomplishments were my own because of who I was and what I was capable of doing, not due to God's influence in my life. And although I tried to act humbly on the outside when people complimented me, I knew deep down that my good deeds were, at least in part, due to me.

At the height of my struggles with trying to find a balance between my active and interior lives, and only seventeen months after my last cancer relapse, I got hit again with another cancer relapse. My alpha-fetoprotein climbed to 895 in August 2000, after it had been totally normal three months earlier around. For our local laboratory at the time, a normal alpha-fetoprotein was below five. A PET scan and CT scan could not find the tumor. By December 2000, we had found a small two-centimeter mass by my left inguinal area. This added some validity to that feeling I'd had in church earlier in the year, when I had a vision during prayer that I was going to have a relapse, and my left pelvic area and left leg were highlighted. It also gave me a sense of comfort that on that day in prayer, God had let me know that I was going to be OK. I had surgery again, and, as I write this chapter in January 2002, I have been in remission for a year.

This last relapse turned out to be another opportunity for spiritual growth. I am coming to appreciate that God sometimes puts us in situations where we are given the opportunity to grow. Some of these situations are relatively easy to handle without much stress. Some situations are a major deal, like a death in the family, an earthquake, or a cancer relapse. In my dark sense of humor, I could visualize God with a big whip, telling me to get down on my knees, ask for forgiveness, and let go of my pride. Down, boy! Down, boy! Bow your head, shrug your shoulders, and feel humble in your heart!

In my theological ignorance, I wonder if the authors of the Old Testament also saw God with a big whip or maybe a lightning bolt. They portrayed God as being very tough and punishing. But deep down inside, I knew God would never want to punish me. It is not God's nature. There are times when God might withdraw from us, especially if we want our will to be in command, but God would never use negative energy to hurt us.

I joked with people around me that this second cancer relapse was another opportunity for personal and spiritual growth. I joked with myself that I hadn't done my homework the right way the first time—mainly being with God and learning how to pray—so I got a second chance to do it. I actually did mean this, but I had no idea how this growth would occur. The more I spoke with people about this, the more I realized that I needed to experience suffering in order to grow.

It is during suffering when I am most vulnerable. My soul is at the mercy of God, and as I pray to God, I draw closer to God. This perceived suffering occurs when I find myself in situations where I want my will to be in command and not let God's will come through.

The surgical experience with this second cancer relapse was certainly different from my first relapse. I was better prepared, spiritually. My praying was more fervent, and I was easily going to church about five to six times a week. Two major events happened during my hospitalization that left me with a very vivid and lasting impression.

The first one had to do with my own mortality and my ability to let go. How many cancer relapses am I going to survive before I kick the bucket? Do I really have any say in my survival? Can I will myself to live? If I do will myself to live, is my will stronger than God's? For the month prior to surgery, I dealt with these questions without any good answers. Regardless, I continued to pray for my health.

As I got closer to surgery day, I felt a humbleness settle in my heart. Although I still willed myself to live—mainly for Anne, Tim, and Patty—I was beginning to accept that God made the final call. I still struggled, to a lesser degree, with trying to reconcile my active and interior lives, but this did not seem as important as dealing with cancer.

How far was I willing to let go? I felt that God and I were having a stare-down. How far was I willing to let go and let God take control before I flinched? About three weeks before surgery, I copied a number of prayers and pasted them into a small booklet that I began to take to church. The Prayer of Abandonment by Fr. Charles de Foucauld[6] became my favorite prayer as I neared surgery:

> My Father,
> I abandon myself to you;
> Make of me what you will.
> Whatever You make of me, I thank you;
> I am ready for everything,
> I accept everything.
> Provided that your will be done in me,
> In all Your creatures,
> I desire nothing else, Lord.
> I put my soul in your hands,
> I give it to you, Lord, with all the love in my heart,
> Because I love you,

And because it is for me a need of love
To give myself,
To put myself in your hands unreservedly,
With definite trust.
For you are my Father.

On the day of surgery, I felt somewhat tense and nervous. Although the probabilities were overwhelming that the surgery would be fine, there was still a possibility that something would go wrong, and perhaps I wouldn't wake up from anesthesia. I just might die on the operating table. Was I ready to die?

The moment of truth came at surgery time. There were multiple attempts to get an IV started, but they could not find a vein. The anesthesiologist finally decided to put me under anesthesia without sedation, as I did not have an IV. After anesthesia, my veins would dilate, and it would be easier to get an IV in.

He placed the mask on my face and asked me to take some deep breaths. It felt a little claustrophobic, having that mask on me, but I decided to relax and simply take deep breaths. Not getting poked for an IV anymore was certainly a reason to relax. The metallic taste of that first breath was not pleasant. The second breath made my head feel light, and my whole body got heavy. I felt like I had had a six-pack of beer in less than a minute. I had the feeling that I was not going to be awake much longer. Knowing the possibility that I might not wake up ever again, I prayed one more time, "Lord, I abandon myself to you." And I let go. It seemed as if I had jumped over a cliff, but there was no gravity pull involved. I became suspended in air, weightless and without worry.

When I woke up, my eyes were still closed, but I could hear nurses by my side, asking me to wake up. The surgery was over, and they asked me to squeeze their hands. Although I felt I was ready to die, it actually felt good to wake up and realize, within a few seconds of surveying my body for normal movement and sensations, that

I was alive. Surgery had gone as expected, and there had been no major complications.

I knew the routine for recovery. From the physical point of view, I knew that the NG tube would be in for a few days, that I needed to get out of bed and start walking as soon as I could to minimize complications, and that I needed to do my incentive spirometer to help open my lungs and not get fevers. The spiritual experience, however, gave me what I consider the second gift from this surgery. The first gift, of course, was realizing that I could let go of my life completely, and God would hold me in the palm of God's hand.

The second gift was feeling God flow through me with love and peacefulness. I can't think of a more awesome experience than this. It was so pure and free of this world that words could not do justice to describing it. I experienced this feeling several times a day during my hospitalization. It typically tended to happen when I was falling asleep for a short nap. Because my sleep patterns were disrupted, I napped during the night as well and had these experiences in the middle of the night. I would say I was in and out of naps during the first seventy-two hours of post-op recovery, and I just kept having these awesome experiences.

This feeling had no visual image or interpretation in my mind. It simply came to me as a surprise or gift. It instilled confidence in me that I would recover without any difficulties.

I also continued to pray in the hospital while I was recovering. When I was awake and alert, I would take my little blue prayer book that I had made prior to surgery and say my list of prayers, sometimes a few times a day. I had a prayer that read, "Lord, place your hand over my body and let your love and energy flow through every cell in my body and into the deepest chambers of my soul." I could visualize God placing God's hand over me and healing me. With time, I have come to appreciate that these two activities were different and very powerful.

The first one almost felt mystical. I had never experienced this before. I have no doubt that this came from God. I have not spoken to a priest to see if this constitutes what the saints would call a supernatural phenomenon. I don't know if morphine had anything to do with these feelings, but I do know that I was more alert and active during the early stages of recovery with this surgery than with other surgeries. I also did not request morphine injections as I had in the past, as I did not feel as much pain. This makes me feel that morphine probably did not play a role with these feelings.

The second activity was more mental and meditative prayer. I read from my prayer book, and I meditated and visualized God healing me. This was a more active form of prayer on my part, although any time we are in prayer, God is very active as well.

Whereas in my previous hospitalizations, I was taking about eleven to fourteen days to recover (including readmissions), this hospitalization lasted only five days. When I came home to recover, I prayed about twice a day with my booklet. After my usual prayers, I quickly led myself into meditation and then into the state of peacefulness and love that I had experienced in the hospital. It was very quiet in my heart and mind. I simply felt peace, love, and joy.

In very crude terms, you could say this behaved like an addiction. Whereas before surgery I wanted to go to church almost every morning, now I craved being with God in prayer throughout the whole day. I sometimes found myself going into prayer several times a day. It helped that the house was quiet for a good part of the day while the kids were at school.

And when Tim and Patty came home, I experienced tremendous joy and thankfulness to be with them. I know this was a difficult time for Anne because I was limited in what I was able to do to help around the house. With time, I gradually increased my level of activity and was able to help her, but Anne knows that I am incredibly thankful for having her on my side.

After having three months off to recover, I went back to work in the spring of 2001. I asked my partners to let me have two-hour lunches so I could come home and rest. To be fair, I took a pay cut as well. With time, I changed my activities during lunchtime, from napping all the time, to writing this book, to sometimes going to mass at noon, to sometimes running.

I must admit that getting back to work has resulted in my inability to feel God like I did during those days after my surgery. Once again, the frustrations, stress, and sadness that can go along with taking care of people have surfaced. However, I have learned to use my will to take care of things where I can make an impact, but I back off and accept that which I cannot change. I have tried to transport that feeling of love and peacefulness to when I enter a room to examine a child. I no longer feel passive-aggressive about matters in the active life—at least most of the time. I definitely am aware that I am human like everybody else, and I do falter from time to time.

I have made a couple of more changes in my lifestyle. I gave up caffeine to help my body relax. I know God is within me all the time, but caffeine, along with my busy schedule, made it difficult for me to feel God's peace and love. During my caffeine days, it was easy for me to have a heart rate around ninety beats per minute. Despite the fact that I ran and played soccer, I still had a high heart rate throughout the day. In contrast, at night and late evening, my heart rate would drop into the sixties and usually fifties by bedtime. Since giving up caffeine, my heart rate during the day is commonly around sixty to seventy. My body does not feel tense when I am trying to pray. I don't think I could have appreciated this difference, had it not been for this last surgery. Now, I am more sensitive and perceptive about how tense or relaxed my body feels.

The second change I made, coupled with giving up caffeine, was learning how to relax. During my recovery time and before going back to work, I decided to meet with a psychologist to teach me how to relax. This psychologist specialized in helping oncology patients learn how to reduce stress and to help them visualize how to fight cancer. I met with him for about five sessions over the course of two months and learned about biofeedback. This was very helpful, and to date, there are times when I call on these powers to help me relax at work and at home.

Despite these changes in my spiritual life, prayer, and body relaxation, I can tell I am still learning how to blend and balance my active life with my interior life. To help me stay in tune with God as much as possible, I have continued to pray twice a day—once in the morning when I drop Tim off at school, and once at night before bedtime. Sometimes, I go to mass at noon because I crave going to mass.

I never envisioned that I would pray this often. I remember, even as recently as three years ago, that I thought that going to church on Sundays, taking Communion, and praying just once a week was enough. Of course, at home we always prayed and thanked God for our meals, but this was a different kind of prayer. It was short—maybe thirty seconds—and was one of gratitude. The prayer that I am doing now is effortless. It does not follow any pattern of set prayers. Sometimes, I am in church for ten minutes, and sometimes, I am there for twenty minutes. Sometimes, I say a vocal prayer and meditate, and sometimes, I seem to go into contemplation, just like I did after my surgery.

I have wondered why these changes have happened to me and why they happened at age forty. I sense that God has drawn me closer, and it seems that I needed to go through these cancer relapses in order to change. I needed to suffer a little to change. This leads me to one more change in my statement for why I live here. While I have been placed in a challenging field, I am here to unite my soul with God, which can happen only by the grace of God. I am not here to master my active life and external world; I am to use them as they challenge me and help me to develop a better interior life. Then, I will have a better home for God to dwell in.

I now can appreciate better the beatitude, "Blessed are the meek, for they shall inherit the earth." In the context that this was written, *meek* stands for those who are willing accept God as their supreme being, who accept God's will, and who have faith that God is right.

*The earth* stands for the active and external world. This is one of those paradoxes in life where the more I try to control something, the harder it is to control it. By becoming meek, I allow God to take control. Things may go my way, but if they don't, that's OK. Perhaps there is another route I need to take because God has other plans.

I also have come to appreciate the beatitude, "Blessed are the poor in spirit, for theirs is the kingdom of God." *Poor* does not simply mean financially poor. People who are financially rich have a lot of possessions. They may even become attached to these possessions. *Poor*, in this beatitude, refers to being "rich" in spiritual possessions. For example, being attached to a project to the extent that it occupies my mind all the time is being rich spiritually. There is not enough spiritual time and space for God. Holding a grudge or being upset is being spiritually rich. Under these circumstances, God cannot dwell in me with peace and love. The kingdom of God cannot come to me when I am spiritually rich.

I am still learning about prayer and about God. I know I have much more to learn. I will continue to pray to God that, by God's grace, God will continue to flow through me and that God will grant me the ability to remain humble so that God's will can be mine. Amen.

# Chapter 7

# A New Journey

*February 2002*

I t could have been any other afternoon on a warm, sunny summer day at our lake cottage in August 2000, but today felt different. As I floated on the water with my life-vest on, I could feel the water engulf my arms, legs, and back as one large warm hug of consolation. The sun beamed radiantly on my face and chest and gave me the nurturing and peace that I had been seeking this entire past month. The rhythmic, gentle knock of the waves on the raft's pontoons created a melodic sound that wanted to put me to sleep.

The scream of joy by the kids as they jumped from the raft into the water gave life to this moment and place, which seemed so isolated from the rest of the world. Even Anne, whose face looked so tired and worn out, managed to crack a smile and a laugh. After helping Anne's dad, Bob, this past month with his dying, it just felt good to take a morning off and try to recharge ourselves emotionally. It was almost as if Bob, also known by his grandchildren as Papa, was giving us a gift before he departed. In fact, I felt his presence that morning at the lake. As I closed my eyes, I could see him smile and feel happy for us. He enjoyed being with the kids, and I could feel his approval that Anne and I were doing a good job of raising them. It was just a brief feeling, a brief moment, that perhaps lasted a couple of seconds, but it was a strong feeling.

After we got done playing in the water and got dressed, Anne talked to her mother to get an update on Bob. That morning, his skin had turned gray and blue, and his breathing had become irregular. It sounded as if he was going to die. As we drove back into town to be with the rest of the family, I wondered if he was really going to die that day.

Sometimes, it is hard to predict when somebody is going to die. I remember when Grandma Murphy was ninety years old and was hospitalized with pneumonia. She had been in the hospital for about a week, and she was not getting better. I opted to fly to New Jersey and visit with her, not knowing for sure if that would be the last time I would see her. We talked about life, death, and God. She felt ready to die and was at peace with herself. Her body looked relaxed, and her face looked old and worn out but without any expression of tension or anxiety. I could tell she felt God's presence and was ready to let go. But she didn't die. She eventually recovered from the pneumonia and went to a nursing home, where, after four months, she then died.

I visited with a priest a month after my visit with Grandma. I was having a difficult time understanding how she could be so ready to die, be so at peace with herself, be so in tune with God, yet not die. His expression of amazement stayed with me more than anything he said at the time. He was so impressed that she had given herself up completely to God, to the point that she was ready to let go and die. But his next point, sounding so simple, painted a picture filled with humility: her will to die had to be put on hold until God felt it was time for her to die.

To reach that spiritual state is no easy feat. After all, Grandma was ninety years old. She finally placed herself in God's hands and said, "Lord, take me." Imagine the love from God that must flow through one's soul to reach that state of renouncing one's will.

Bob was sixty-five years old when he died on that sunny, peaceful day, August 15, 2000. About five weeks before, he had been diagnosed with pancreatic cancer. Unfortunately, after a liver ultrasound and an abdominal CT scan, he already had multiple metastases in the liver. The prognosis was not good at all. Chemotherapy could prolong life for another six to twelve months, but at this stage of the game, pancreatic cancer is almost 100 percent fatal. He opted to make the journey toward God, to rest in God's arms and be at peace, thus forgoing surgeries and chemotherapy.

As a physician, I have had several opportunities to participate in patients' dying processes. I saw nursing home residents die when I was in college and medical school, and I saw children die when I was a pediatric resident and physician. But helping Bob die seemed different. I had developed a long relationship with him, and this seemed too personal. It also seemed too close to my life, as I was only fifteen months past my first cancer relapse and surgery. Little did I know that I was about to have my second relapse with cancer just days after burying Bob.

I have come to befriend death and the process of dying, but this was not the case when I was in college. I remember when a soccer teammate was diagnosed with Hodgkin's lymphoma. My concept of cancer at that time was so black-and-white. I thought the diagnosis of lymphoma meant he was going to die. Being close to him, as a friend and soccer teammate, I felt threatened as well. The walls of invincibility during our teenage years didn't seem strong enough anymore. The mood of our team was mixed; we were a soccer team that needed to practice and win games, but the undercurrent flowed with feelings of insecurity and being scared of death. Mike did well with his treatments and later came back to school in good health.

I took religion classes in college as a prerequisite to graduation. As I learned more about God, I deepened my faith in my religion. Although I felt I had a relationship with God that came from the heart, my thoughts prevailed over my heart when I encountered difficult situations. It was all very rational. And when it came to my own mortality, I reasoned that I would accept death when the moment came because this was noble; it was God's way, and no further questions needed to be asked.

This concept stayed with me throughout my second year of medical school. As I was diagnosed with cancer at the end of that school year, I reasoned that I had led a good life, that God had taken good care of me, and now it was time for me to go. As I went through my surgeries and chemotherapy, I developed a fighting spirit that helped me pull through the summer and fall. My will had taken over. Had I defied God?

I had heard that one could not die unless one consented to die. Perhaps I was still alive through my will. But I felt miserable after my first cancer relapse in 1998. I was hanging on to life too hard and had become restless. There was no way I was going to leave Anne and the kids by themselves. Something had to give, and it seemed that it had become a battle of wills: mine versus God's.

I saw my second relapse in 2000 as a failed homework assignment. I hadn't gotten it right with the first relapse in 1998, so I had to do it all over again. But the second time around was different. I felt like I had died with this second relapse. As I prayed to God right before general anesthesia, "Lord, into your hands I commend my soul," I let go, and I placed myself in God's palm so God could have complete control over me. Spiritually, I felt different with this surgical recovery, as I was at peace with myself and with God. During my recovery, I went in and out of dreamlike states, where no words were spoken, but there were simply feelings and images—dreams and images that helped me appreciate my family, my role as a pediatrician, my friends, and soccer. But there were also images or dreams of issues that I needed to work on in order to purify my soul so that God could dwell in me more. There were issues of pride, impatience, lack of charity and love, of unkindness, of contempt and looking down at people. And there were times where I felt that God had initiated the prayer, and I just felt love and peace. These experiences were not premeditated; they happened as I lay in bed. Sometimes they would happen after a prayer, sometimes when I felt I had been completely asleep, and sometimes when I felt half awake and half asleep.

These dreamlike states left me hungry for more. Although the issues sounded negative, there was an associated state of peace, joy, and love. My yearning to be with God had never been so strong. I felt that I had been magnetized toward God, and nobody could pull me away. Through these feelings and dreams, I felt it did not matter if I died. I had experienced, through God's love and presence, that Anne and the kids would be fine without me. They would have their trials, their ups and downs, but in the end, God would always be there with them. This was perhaps the best feeling to have as I contemplated death. I needed to know that they would be fine.

I find it interesting how I have grown in my relationship with God. At first, as a child and young teen, I felt with my heart that God was with me, and I would humble myself when it was time to die. Through my college and medical school years, I reasoned that it would be the right thing to do if God called me, but I couldn't feel it in my heart like I had in the earlier years. Now, twenty years later, I can feel God again in my heart, and I can let go with my heart. I can accept death with humility, but I don't know if I have the humility that Grandma and Bob exhibited before their deaths.

The tricky part is to know when to let go when it is time to go. To date, I practice letting go in church when I'm praying, trying to recollect that feeling when I received anesthesia, right before I fell asleep. But what if I encounter a situation where I am not supposed to die? Should I still let go, or should I fight?

As I write this chapter, I am learning that I don't have to will much to go through life. In between the Prayer of Saint Francis and the Prayer of Abandonment by Charles de Foucauld, I am allowing God to chip away slowly at my will so that God's being will reside better in my soul. I have a long way to go. God knows this, and God is patient with me. I also frequently ask for forgiveness and humility because I frequently fall short of God's will. In a way, I am dying slowly. My will is dying slowly. And as this happens, I can feel God's will filling the void. I can feel God's will through my actions of charity and in everyday life events.

This change seems to be occurring slowly and subtly. This change seems to be active on both my part and God's part. I find myself praying twice a day, sometimes three times a day. I yearn to be with God all the time and have God flow through me. If you asked me twenty years ago if I would be this fanatical about God and religion, I would have answered that I was not that crazy. But these life events with cancer have changed me. And these changes appear to be happening effortlessly. I sit down to pray without much effort, just as when I feel thirsty and get a drink of water from the kitchen faucet. A quick impulse leads to action.

I am finally learning not to be selfish with this good feeling that God gives me during times of prayer and during good deeds. It is tempting to seek prayer so that I can get this good feeling. These consolations are God's way of letting me know that God is with me. But I am learning not to pray so that I can get this good feeling, either in church or at home. I crave that good feeling, and I crave being with God. But if God chooses to give me this feeling, then I accept it. It is God's will that I have this feeling.

But there have been times when I have not felt these consolations, and thus, I am learning to pray for God and not for me. I pray and honor God because God deserves it. It is the least that I can do to honor God.

As I look at death one more time, I view it as a transition event before joining God completely. I live here to encounter life events that become opportunities for personal and spiritual growth. Through these processes, I can purify my soul so that it becomes a better house for God. I am learning to accept, with humility, that God will place me in situations where I can practice God's way of life. The more I can let God's will flow through me, the easier my transition will be when death arrives.

# Chapter 8

# Epilogue, Part 1

*April 2002*

I had two religion classes during college, the New Testament and Origins of Christian Thought. I enjoyed the intellectually stimulating conversations and discussions during class. I also deepened my faith in God and learned more about God's ways. One of my professors made a comment once that stayed with me: "I hope I never stop learning because the day I do, I will cease to live."

Learning has taken on many forms and styles for me. There has been the learning of academics in the classroom, the learning on how to practice medicine and become a pediatrician, and the learning about people's behavior and psychology through life's events, to name a few examples. Learning about God and God's ways has been a lifetime journey, an evolution of my soul, a human relationship on my part and a supernatural relationship on God's part.

There have been some key elements in my continuing effort to improve my relationship with God. First and foremost, as the base of my evolution, is maintaining and further developing my faith in God. I have read about God through the years but definitely more so over the past couple of years, as God has touched me deeply with my cancer relapses. I have learned a fair amount about God, but I feel there is so much more to learn about God. As God is so perfect, with attributes that go beyond my capacity to learn and comprehend, I don't think I will ever attain perfect faith and knowledge of God while I am still here on earth.

Nevertheless, I read and meditate daily about God and Jesus. I have been very intrigued by the saints and how their relationships with God evolved. I am not reading directly from the Bible; I have been relying on the priests to explain the meaning of these passages during mass. This isn't meant to minimize the fruit that can be derived from reading the Bible, but I feel I don't have enough knowledge to understand it by myself at this stage in my life. In the evening, I have read and meditated from *Divine Intimacy*[7] by Father Gabriel of St. Mary Magdalen, OCD. This book contains excerpts from the daily mass Bible readings and a colloquy for each day.

The second key element has been my daily prayer. As I said before, I usually pray twice a day and sometimes a third time, if I go to mass at noon. This praying usually takes about fifteen to twenty minutes, but sometimes I wish it was longer. I am probably being selfish because of the consolations that God gives me during these times. I am tempted to pray sometimes because of the good feeling that I get from God, rather than trying to honor God. Nevertheless, I accept this feeling from God and thank God. I do spend some time during my prayer in thanking God for my health, my family, my work, and so forth. I also spend some time asking for favors. But I would say the bulk of my time in prayer is trying to connect with God; to feel God's love and peace; to feel God's charity, humility, purity of heart and wisdom. I also try to feel, based on Saint Louis de Montfort's *True Devotion to Mary*, Jesus's agony in the garden and how to have contempt for sin, or Jesus's scourging by the pillars and how I can mortify my senses. All these surgeries and the experiences of pain and discomfort associated with them have allowed me to understand that it is possible to mortify my senses so that I can disregard these and move forward. Our connection with God is one that does not involve our bodies, and therefore it is good to learn how to disregard these distractions that come from our senses.

This is difficult to do, and I do not claim to be an expert at it. I am still learning about prayer and feel that I have a long way to go. A book that I found helpful was *An Introduction to the Devout Life*,[8] published in 1609, by Saint Francis de Sales (1567–1622). The first chapters focus on prayer, and he gives the reader specific guidance on how to pray. Although his writings started out as letters of counsel to Madame de Charmoisy in France, these writings were put together in book format, and it now comes across as a book written for us laypeople, who don't have a vocation in the clergy. It is written with the understanding of our busy lives, with all the joys and stresses of life. One of my favorite sayings from his book is, "Everyone of us needs half an hour of prayer every day, except when we are busy— then we need an hour." The next book I plan to read is *The Way of Perfection*[9] by Saint Teresa of Avila (1515–1582). My understanding is that this book is also good for learning how to pray.

The third element in my effort to improve my relationship with God has been my understanding and acceptance of death. I have come to accept, with my heart and soul and not just my mind, that my life here on earth is finite. Someday, it will be my time to leave and unite my soul with God. This has been difficult to accept, as there are times when I do will myself to live—probably, God is letting me live. I don't know how I am going to react when death is imminent, but if it's looking obvious that I am going to die, I will probably let go and place myself in God's hands. I think this feeling comes close to that experience prior to my last surgery. Spiritually, I continue to try to die every day, so as to let God's will flow through me. Again, I can't claim to do an outstanding job at this, but I am trying. I feel that God is patient with me and understands my human nature and propensity to make mistakes.

By acknowledging and accepting death, I have come to appreciate living every day to its fullest. I have nothing to lose and everything to gain. When I talk about gains, I refer to those opportunities for personal and spiritual growth, those opportunities that will allow me to get closer to God. While it is important to take care of the active life and those active works, in the end, it is my interior life that will lead me down the path that will allow for this union.

All of this leads me to my last key element. I need to have humility and accept God as the skipper of my voyage. I need to accept that God will purify my soul in God's own time and on God's own terms. There have been times when I have felt impatient in wanting to develop further my interior life. My strong desire to be close to God has led me to situations where I wanted to exert my will and force my relationship with God, including testing myself to see how close I was getting to God. But I have learned to back off and let God take the reins.

This humility has also been important in helping me understand that I have a long way to go in my spiritual development. Two sources have been good in helping me understand where I stand with God.

*The Interior Castle*,[10] also known as *The Seven Mansions*, was written by Saint Teresa of Avila in 1577. This book was so difficult for me to read that I had to use an analysis by Father Jordan Aumann, a Carmelite priest who is still active in giving lectures in Georgia. This book was inspired by a vision that Saint Teresa had from God. There was a crystal globe in the soul containing seven concentric mansions, with the innermost mansion being at the highest level and being the brightest. This innermost mansion had a throne and the king of glory, God. The outside of the castle was filled with venomous snakes, toads, and vipers. Within each mansion, there were rooms where the soul was allowed to roam about at will. Each mansion, as it moved inward and upward, represented advancement in spiritual life. God helps the soul move or progress into more advanced mansions, but the soul also has a will, and sometimes it might digress to a lower mansion.

A soul that is in a state of mortal sin is not allowed in the castle.

The first mansion, therefore, has many people in a state of grace, but they live mostly in the active or exterior life. Their prayers are mainly vocal and usually not fervent. By contrast, a soul in the seventh mansion is very active in the interior life, and its prayer is described as a "prayer of union," a mystical marriage between the soul and God, where the soul is absorbed into the divine. I envision the saints being at this level.

The second source that has helped me understand where I am with my development has been *The Soul of the Apostolate* by Father Jean-Baptiste Chautard. The first manuscript or pamphlet was released in 1907, and this eventually became the cornerstone or basis for his book. Based on whether the soul commits mortal sin, venial sin, or has imperfections, as well as based on the type of prayer in which it engages, the soul can be found in one of nine levels of spiritual development. The descriptions of each level parallel those in Saint Teresa of Avila's *The Seven Mansions*.

Regardless of the source, the general feeling that I get is that I have made some progress, but I have a long way to go. These two books were good to satisfy my curiosity but, in the end, my level does not matter because God will perfect my soul on God's own terms and time. I appreciate that God can reveal only so much to me of what lies ahead. The upper-level mansions look so wonderful that I am tempted to leave this world, knowing that Anne and the kids will be fine, and unite my soul with God. The problem with this line of thinking is that it is not my prerogative to make the call as to when my life should end. In addition, I get the feeling that the more we advance ourselves while here on earth, the more spiritually mature we will be to handle the divine world and, therefore, rest in better peace.

I also find it interesting that God can show me only so many trials at a time. There have been times when I have felt tired and disconsolate with some of my hardships. God never intends for us to suffer, but God uses these hardships for us to lean on God, improve on our prayer, improve in our faith, and get closer to God. God will only give me as much as God knows I can handle, even though my perception of the hardship might be overwhelming.

Thus, with humility, I pray to God that God continues to help me to line up my will with God's will, that I abandon myself completely so that I may place my soul in the palm of God's hand, and that I may be an instrument of God's peace so that God's works of charity may be carried out through me. Amen.

# Part 2

Part 2

# Chapter 9

# Trying to Connect with God

*November 2007*

I have not died. The last time I wrote was in 2002, and, by God's mercy and love, I find myself still alive. I was convinced that after having a couple of cancer relapses, I was on my way to dying, but this did not happen. Instead, I have tried to develop a relationship with God that has had many ups and downs.

I have continued to do a fair amount of reading about the saints over the past five years. Reading about them has given me some understanding of their struggles as they tried to get close to God, thus giving me some understanding for my current struggles. Also, their writings have illuminated a path for me to follow. If they could become one with God, then maybe I can do that too. Their writings give me courage and a sense of hope that I too can go in that direction.

I also met Father Fitz in 2005 and began a relationship of meeting with him monthly, except during the month of June, when he goes to Nebraska to serve as a spiritual director to the seminarians while they are in their retreat. I have found these meetings very helpful, as I frequently become anxious from trying to improve my relationship with God while constantly doing things my way. I become impatient and want my relationship with God to be instantaneously better. Father Fitz has been instrumental in pointing out where I am misinterpreting God's love and when I have failed to see God's love. In a very kind way, he has pointed out when my will was strong and was taking over and how I could have given way to God. I always walk away from our meetings with a sense of peace and love from God.

Perhaps another reason why I have not written in a while is that I have been in a state of spiritual confusion and have not been sure where I was going in my relationship with God. I guess with today's writing, this becomes a good opportunity to vent a little.

I find myself frequently frustrated because I don't feel God with me all the time. There is no question in my mind that God is with me all the time, but it is of my own doing that I don't let God in. There are times when I feel God's presence through affections and consolations, but there are times when I find myself too busy with the active life to be able to maintain communication with God. During these times I find that my communication, mainly through prayer, is weak.

I wonder sometimes if the saints had this problem too, going back and forth between the active life and interior life. I wonder if they thought the easier path was to renounce the active life, become hermits, or isolate themselves in a monastery so that they could be with God all the time. But my gut feeling tells me that I need the challenges in life—the exterior world or active life, if you will—to allow me to develop spiritually, the interior world.

The saints that I have read about and learned about seemed to be active in the exterior world. They were able to maintain a good attitude, a good course or path with God; they were able to sustain all the adversity that came with the active life. Both Saint Teresa of Avila and Saint John of the Cross come to mind. I think their prayer must have been very strong. They must have been very meek and humble to deal with adverse events in life, which then became exercises to allow them to become even more meek and humble. In doing so, they were able to allow God to come into them better and then carry out God's works better.

I seem to develop a state of complacency in my prayer in communicating with God. When things are going well, I don't even work very hard at meekness and humility. I can tell that my prayer becomes lukewarm. But when adversity shows up, I struggle initially in the active life by trying to make things better by myself. I become impatient and intolerant, and I lack love and charity. If I don't appear to act like this outwardly, at a minimum I feel it inside, in my heart. After time passes, I am able to reconcile and recollect myself through God's grace, and I am able to go back to being humble. At that point, my connection with God improves, and I feel God's affection and consolation.

I feel frustrated when I realize that I have gone back and forth between the active life and interior life and how this affects my prayer in connection with God. Very slowly, I have started to realize that I need to recognize God's presence in everything and everybody that surrounds me. It seems that only in constantly acknowledging God's presence in everything and everybody can I deal better with the active life. In fact, by acknowledging God's presence, I am able to prepare better, even when there is a storm. I wonder if this is how the saints were able to be with God in both the active and interior lives, and thus, they were able to feel peace and love constantly while connected to God.

It has not been easy, trying to change this attitude or direction in life. I feel that I have to make a strong mental effort to acknowledge God's presence in everything and everybody. This process in my current state of spiritual development has not happened in a seamless way. I have to put mental effort into it.

Aren't we all impatient at times? Don't we get frustrated when things don't go our way, or we can't make things better on our own? We want things fixed right away, to be made better instantaneously.

But God understands our impatience. I can feel Jesus saying to us, "Give me your impatience, and I will make you whole. I will help you understand that I am here for you, forever and ever. I have the time to be with you, and together, we can work on this. I am present in everything visible and invisible. Come be by me; abide by me." I then take a deep breath, exhale, and rest quietly.

# Chapter 10

# What Does Freedom Mean to You?

*January 2008*

Father Fitz posed a question to me late last fall—"What does freedom mean to you?—and I didn't have an answer at the time that satisfied me. As I meditated on this concept through the fall season, the best that I could come up with was what it felt like when I went out for runs.

I remembered late August 2007, when the temperature hovered between eighty and ninety degrees. The birds were chirping on that clear-sky morning, the wind was sleeping, and the roads were peaceful. The fresh air brought life into my lungs, and it seemed like it was a good day for a long run. I had given up playing soccer for a few years and decided to focus on my running. My weekly running mileage had been increasing over the summer, and the "long runs" on the weekends had become my challenge!

I gradually had built up my mileage without any major injuries and intended to run eight miles that day. Averaging about ten minutes per mile, I figured I would be gone for a little less than 1.5 hours. I'd done seven miles the previous weekend, and that was a good mental preparation for that day. The first mile was usually my warm-up mile, where my muscles loosened up, and then, somewhere between the second and third mile, all the aches and pains would go away as I hit my rhythm. By the fourth and fifth mile, my legs would start to get a hint of tiredness, but at that point, my run felt efficient. The lifting of my thigh followed smoothly with the contraction of the opposite calf, which resulted in a kick that briefly suspended me in the air. One step after another carried a rhythm that was free of the awkward running that was present at the beginning. The kicking, the breathing, and the arm movements were effortless and devoid of any pain. Even my heart purred comfortably without causing any shortness of breath.

It was during these middle miles and before the last mile, when exhaustion would set in, that I experienced physical freedom. I could run far away and not feel dragged down by the discomfort that was present at the beginning of the run. I actually felt that I could conquer these chains of physical stiffness, aches, and inefficient running that seemed so heavy at the start of the run. It was also during these miles that my mind detached itself from this world, as I became focused on my running, attempting to achieve and maintain that effortless rhythm. The thoughts and anxieties of the day, along with my awkward running, vanished when I hit my stride, and my mind popped through the sky as I became suspended in air, worry-free and without any anxiety about injuries or muscle stiffness.

Although I experience this physical freedom on a regular basis, it is the spiritual freedom that has been elusive. When I pray, "God grant me the grace to experience your freedom," what am I actually asking?

We were born to be free but free of what? When I am running, I experience freedom when I hit my stride, and I detach myself from the awkward mental and physical running that was present at the beginning of my run. But in the spiritual world, what am I trying to detach myself from these days?

It appears that anxieties and frustrations still hang around my daily life. Despite recognizing these awkward feelings for quite some time as obstacles to the union of my soul with God and praying to God to help me deal with these feelings, to help me be more patient, it has hit me recently that I am putting emphasis on these feelings of anxiety and frustration and not dealing with the root of the issue or circumstance. I am trying to fix—or asking God to help me fix—a consequence, when, in reality, I should be dealing with the root. I am asking God to help me get rid of the anxieties and frustrations but not figuring out what has been causing those anxieties and frustrations.

Anxieties and frustrations commonly happen when my will is not getting its way. My will continues to be very strong still, in a way that is not completely meek and humble. I am not open-minded enough of God's divine providence and have not learned to recognize that I am dependent on God. Father Fitz explained to me that I am carrying things that God wants me to give up, little by little. These possessions can be frustrations from not getting my way at work, impatience at not seeing enough good outcomes, worrying about myself and not giving out charity and love to others, being envious, or worrying about how to improve myself in soccer or in running. And because they seem to be possessions that I treasure, they almost appear as little trophies that I hang on to. But very slowly, God is asking me to give up these trophies, including the smallest one of all, whichever that might be.

I do not know how big this little trophy is that I am still carrying around and that God wants me to hand over. At a minimum, today I can say that pride is one of those trophies that I need to hand over. Humility, the opposite of pride, allows me to see myself as I truly am, with all my positive qualities but also negative attributes. I am no bigger or smaller than what I currently am. I am sure I have other little trophies to hand over to God.

Don't we all hang on to trophies or possessions that seem to create some sense of comfort in us? They are part of us. It's almost like they create a false sense of security in us and help us stay the way we are. And if we are to give these up, we would feel a little naked because they have helped define who we are. But God is asking us to give up these frustrations from work or home; these worries about our health and how we are performing; these false senses of identity through our pride.

Perhaps I can pray to God to help me hit my spiritual stride and help me get rid of these possessions. Nothing would make me happier than if God granted me the ability to be a good servant, an instrument of peace and love, by being freer. I must continue to die to myself by giving up these possessions through God's grace so that God can live through me. I need to die to myself by putting aside my passions and my strong will so that I can sense God's will better. In that way, I can be open to God's divine providence in a meek and humble way and be God's servant, all for the honor and glory of God and not for me.

Thank you, God, for giving me the gift of running. Through running, I can experience physical freedom, which allows me to visualize what spiritual freedom could be like. By detaching myself from these possessions—what seem to be trophies that I am hanging on to—I can let your Holy Spirit flow through me and help me be one with you.

# Chapter 11

# Losing Faith

*April 2008*

The end of 2007 and beginning of 2008 was a period of frustration with a sense of failure, as it related to work. As we got closer to Easter Sunday, I found myself in prayer and meditating on Jesus carrying his cross in Calvary.

I could see myself carrying a cross and going up a hill. Every step I took got heavier and slower. The sweat on my forehead dripped into my eyes and made it harder for me to see. My mouth felt dry, and the air was hot. I continued to look down, but from the corners of my eyes, I could make out the silhouettes of people as they lined the dirt road in silence and watched me make my way up the hill.

As I took a bend on the road, I thought about the pain caused by the politics of practicing medicine. I was the medical director of research for our organization and had also become the pediatric hospitalist medical director for one of the local community hospitals. The responsibilities were heavy, and the number of people that I had to work with was large.

Fighting hard against the grain, I found myself slowly succumbing to the negativity of work. I carried the stress and negativity of work to my family relationships at home. In the middle of the long Michigan winter, I found myself always pressed for time. It seemed that there was not enough time in the late afternoon to pick up my kids from school, get them to their guitar or violin lessons, help them with their homework, take them to tennis lessons, cook dinner, and take the dog outside to go potty.

My prayer life had begun to feel like a bent stick that was about to break. The stresses and busyness of life were wearing me down. I tried to look at these challenges as opportunities to grow, personally and spiritually. I thought that these could be opportunities to humble myself further and to let God flow through me. But the winter season had grown long, and I felt the need to gain control of my life. I began to debate, although it seemed in a somewhat repressed way, if perhaps I was sinning or was about to sin by pushing God to the side so that I could go back to the old way of doing things, where I was in control and God was a bystander.

As I finished taking the bend in the road and looked ahead, there seemed to be much dirt and stone ahead of me. It was almost noon, and the sun was beating hard on my body. As I visualized Jesus receiving lashings from the Roman guards, I too felt the muscle aches and pain on my skin from the earlier lashings that seemed too much to bear. For one long second, I wondered if I could go on any farther up this road. I wondered if I could regenerate the strength in my thighs to continue uphill. And then, in an instant that was thoughtless and liberating, I fell to the ground on my knees and let this heavy wooden cross that I was carrying on my back and shoulders fall to the ground. It was almost one week before the Lenten season would be over and Easter Sunday would arrive. Some in the crowd simply looked at me, as if perhaps they were empathizing with me. Others wanted to help me get up, but there was nothing there. There was no strength, only pain and exhaustion.

Out of survival instinct and falling way short of what Mother Teresa would have done, I simply stood up, without picking up my cross. I looked at the people to my right and excused myself as I made my way through the crowd and down the partly grassy hill.

"I am done," I said to myself and to God as tears began to roll down my cheeks, and I escaped what seemed to be a stage play.

I did not feel God's presence anymore and could not rely on God anymore to help me make decisions at work or at home. I needed to make straightforward, quick decisions with common sense. I did not want to soul-search anymore for what God was trying to tell me. I needed to part with this chaotic, confused, spiritual world of trying to be a leader in my medical field and a dad at home, while trying to be humble and meek.

My acknowledging that I am small and so dependent on God has been a process that I have been letting God work on me for a number of years. This process, however, has been hard and long and has required much patience.

This imagery in prayer, as I entered Holy Week, led to my next thoughts of Jesus doing the Sermon of the Mount. In Matthew 4, Jesus has started his ministry by selecting his disciples and curing those in need. In Matthew 5, Jesus brought his disciples together and delivered to them what we call the *beatitudes*—eight general principles that have become a cornerstone in Christian spirituality. One of these seemed very pertinent to what I was going through at the time: "Blessed are the meek, for they will inherit the earth" (Matthew 5:5).

I read *The Sermon of the Mount*[11] by Emmet Fox, and he gives a good explanation of these beatitudes. He describes the word *meek*:

> It is a mental attitude for which there is no single
> word available, and it is this mental attitude which
> is the secret of prosperity or success in prayer. It is
> a combination of open-mindedness, faith in God,
> and the realization that the Will of God for us is
> always something joyous and interesting and vital,
> and much better than anything we could think

of ourselves. ... This state of mind also includes a perfect willingness to allow this Will of God to come about in whatever way Divine Wisdom considers best, rather than in some particular way that we have chosen for ourselves.

The word *earth* in this biblical context, and as was intended by Jesus, means more than just looking at the land. As Fox explains,

The word earth ... really means manifestation ... as the result of a cause ... and all causation is mental ... all your affairs—your home, your business, all your experience—are but the manifestation of your mental states. [In other words,] your "earth" means the whole of your experience, and to "inherit the earth" means to have dominion over that outer experience; that is to say, to have power to bring your conditions of life into harmony and true success.

Learning how to be meek has been very difficult for me. Being open-minded and having faith in God's divine providence so that I may inherit the earth is one of the great paradoxes of life. Inheriting the earth implies, to me, that I may have dominion over what is around me. But how can I have dominion over everything around me not by exercising my will to have dominion over everything but by letting God exercise God's strength and will?

I frequently find myself in leadership positions, not because I want to be but because people around me think I should be. I wonder, in retrospect, if I was seduced by their words and compliments and felt obliged to become a leader. I have been trying to practice meekness so that a task can be completed well, particularly in God's eyes. A leader needs to know his territory ahead and have some control, some dominion, over his land, his earth. He needs to have vision and inherit that earth to help the group move ahead. Yet as

Jesus described it in his Sermon on the Mount, this inheritance of the earth has to happen while being open-minded to God's divine providence. I need to know what God wants so that I can be God's instrument. I have a difficult time with praying in a meek and humble way when life is too fast-paced and stressful. I eventually fall.

As we headed toward Easter Sunday, I found myself still hurt and alone. I had been stuck in my own decision-making world, without talking much to God lately. During Holy Week, however, I found the pressures from work and home were gone. A lot of my decision-making that week had been in letting go, no matter how much discomfort and pain God was letting happen to me. I was simply tired of it all, and just like in my prayer and meditation, I let go of my cross, stood up, and walked away. Because I felt that God was involved in all this, I had a difficult time reconciling with God, even after receiving the sacrament of reconciliation later that week. In the Catholic faith, reconciliation, or penance (also known as confession), is a sacrament where our sins are absolved by the priest, and in obtaining forgiveness, we can reconcile with God and with the church.

It took the following week, during spring break on the sunny beaches of the Gulf Coast of Florida, before I began to feel the pull toward God again. I wanted to make the relationship better, but the words were not coming out from me. I had not done my daily prayer in two weeks, and I felt awkward saying something. I felt that I needed to say to God that I was sorry but wasn't sure if I was honestly sorry. I wanted God to make it better, to infuse me with God's love, but I wasn't sure how to meet God halfway.

Spring break coincided with Easter Sunday that year, and we chose to go to Marco Island, as we had several times before. I am not sure what attracts me so much to San Marco Church on Marco Island. There is the Spanish-style architecture with the clay-shingle roof. I also like the red-and-white garments the altar boys wear for mass. There's always the guy who plays the trumpet in the choir, playing strong, pure tones despite his older age. But that day, it was the gospel reading of the two disciples walking to Emmaus (Luke 24:13–35) that got my attention.

Jesus had died on the cross, and many had been left disheartened and disillusioned—solemn, you could say—at the thought that who they thought was the Messiah had been killed. Two of the disciples had left Jerusalem and were walking back to the town of Emmaus when they encountered a stranger who wanted to walk with them. Little did they know that it was Jesus who ended up walking with them, "but they were kept from recognizing him" (Luke 24:16). They felt sad, perhaps somewhat depressed, that Jesus had died even though he was supposed to be their Savior. Their hope seemed to have vanished. The concept of the Resurrection, just like with the other disciples, eluded them. But they let their love, kindness, and fellowship come through as they invited this stranger to dine with them and spend the evening together. And then, with the breaking of the bread, they lifted their faces and recognized Jesus.

From this reading, I came to appreciate that God reveals himself only in as much as we are able to understand him, comprehend his nature, and recognize him in the moment. For the disciples, their lack of faith at the beginning of their walk with Jesus did not allow them to recognize Jesus as he was. But when Jesus offered himself in the breaking of the bread—something that was familiar to them and engulfed with love—they then recognized him. Jesus met them where they were.

I must admit my faith in God was weakened through the busy life and stresses of the day. Don't we all seem to lose our ability to believe that God can help us out, even in the direst of situations, just as I found myself prior to Holy Week? Despite praying daily, which, in retrospect, was lukewarm, I lost my compass to the world of humility and meekness. But when we let go of all those attachments of resentment, impatience, anger, and disappointment—that which constitute the land or the earth—meekness and humility begin to surface again. And at the same time, as we show love for those around us, we recognize that God is flowing through us. God helps us raise our faces and helps us recognize God's true nature one more time.

God is patient with us and recognizes that we seem to fall often, yet God's love always finds a way to make things better. As the two disciples recounted on that day, and to paraphrase Luke 24:32, I too find myself saying, "Was not my heart burning within me while he spoke to me?" I may not have recognized God being with me all the time while I went through my struggles, but that itching that I had in my heart to want to talk with God again, even if I did not know how to make things better, was actually God calling me to be in relationship with God again. My heart was burning with God trying to reach out to me.

As I finish writing this chapter, I feel my heart flaming with joy and peace. I am experiencing God so much at this moment that I wonder if I need to make a radical change in my life so that I can be with God more.

Thank you, God, for your continuing unconditional love and patience. Thank you for the gift of faith and for helping us develop it further, helping us to believe in you. You can come in the oddest ways, when we don't recognize you initially, but you lift our faces to help us see you, and in the breaking of the bread, we can then recognize you. Thank you, God, for setting our hearts on fire to help us better appreciate being with you. Maybe then can we be better instruments of your peace and love.

# Chapter 12

# A Letter to God: I Long for You

*February 2009*

The past six months have been marked by a fervent love for God. I find myself often feeling God's love and peace, even in the midst of a busy day, where before, I used to get stressed and anxious. I think some of this may be related to the continued reading of the saints but also from a couple of videos that I have watched on Cistercian monks and cloistered nuns. Their lifestyle and quietness appeal to me, to the point that it has made me at times wonder what it would be like to be in a monastery. This brought me to one afternoon where I found myself in prayer, contemplating a monk at work.

It was early morning, and there was a slight chill to the air. The sky was mostly black, with a hint of blue in the horizon. The crickets rubbed their legs together while the birds chirped at random. The monk's toes got wet from the dew on the grass as he walked out to the field for another day of hard labor. His cloak covered his mostly bald head, and the long brown sleeves gave him warmth. The slow but determined pace of his walk allowed him to work out the stiffness in his joints after sitting and kneeling in his room and, later, in church for the past three hours. This was going to be another glorious day for the elder monk with round-rimmed glasses and a gray-black beard.

His routine has been the same, day after day. He wakes up at three in the morning and prays in his room before going to church and meeting in silence with his fellow monks. He tends the fields throughout the day and assists with the collection and sorting of eggs from the chicken farm. All along, while he works silently, he is actively in prayer with God. The hard physical labor allows him to center his mind and heart in God. At times, he speaks to God in his mind; at others, he simply rejoices in being a servant. But most of the time, this Trappist monk feels God's presence and basks in his peace and love.

The imagery in my prayer has given me an opportunity to see myself as a monk as I contemplate my relationship with God and reflect on my daily prayer life. I continue further with my prayer. Perched on a tree not far from the monastery, I have been watching this elder monk for a few months. I am intrigued by his day-in/day-out work ethic. He maintains a constant pace and does not appear to be distracted by the birds or the dogs chasing the chickens, by the heat of midday, or by his brother monk struggling with the plow. He does not complain of the work that lies ahead but rejoices in it as a new day to be with God.

I have wondered about God's divine providence for me. I acknowledge that God created me in God's image, and I understand that God intervenes in my life to help me actualize who I am going to be. In divine providence, God takes care of me and cooperates with everything that happens to me and surrounds me, directing me, eventually, to become or actualize the person that God intended for me to be.

I have wondered if my next step in getting closer to God

will require a radical change in my life, where I would join the monastery. There, I could be silent and speak only with God. Oh Lord, how I long to be with you, but my prayer is so weak, and I feel so incomplete and selfish that even my heart is not ready to receive you.

I read Psalm 63, and this prayer, for a brief moment, allows me tune out my outside world and simply be closer to you:

> You, God, are my God,
> earnestly I seek you;
> I thirst for you,
> my whole being longs for you,
> in a dry and parched land
> where there is no water.
>
> I have seen you in the sanctuary
> and beheld your power and your glory.
> Because your love is better than life,
> my lips will glorify you.
> I will praise you as long as I live,
> and in your name I will lift up my hands.
> I will be fully satisfied as with the richest of foods;
> with singing lips my mouth will praise you.
>
> On my bed I remember you;
> I think of you through the watches of the night.
> Because you are my help,
> I sing in the shadow of your wings.
> I cling to you;
> your right hand upholds me.

But in your divine providence, you have placed me in this world to be with my family, whom I love very much, and to be a pediatrician, taking care of children and their parents. The work, day in and day out, at times seems like a challenge and frequently reveals my weaknesses: impatience, selfishness, bad temper, and short in love and charity. With all the activity going on around me, I sometimes find it difficult to connect with you. But lately, you have treated me with a soft hand and bathed me in consolations.

I would love to be isolated in the monastery, where I could pray constantly and be with you. The elder monk does not seem to have distractions and maintains an even pace throughout the day. But as I reflect on my day, from the early morning, when I get up, to late at night, when my daughter goes to bed, I realize that I have a full day of activity, just like the monk does. But I find your presence differently than the monk; I see you in the innocence and purity of heart in the newborn baby and in the smiles of the new mother and father. I see you in the child who is ill and receives consolation as I lay my hand on her forehead. I see your freedom of spirit as I laugh at my daughter's sense of humor. I see you trying to burst out of my teenage son's heart as he tries to find his identity as you created him. I see you in my wife as we share our love for each other. But most of all, I see myself as your servant as I try to help wherever and whenever I am needed, and that brings joy to my heart and soul.

Then I realize that, perhaps, my monastery is right here and right now. The work is laid out for me from the early morning until late at night. I try as best as I can to acknowledge your presence in everything and everybody that surrounds me, and I talk with you constantly throughout the day, as I feel your divine providence. My shortcomings are different from the elder monk's, but I am sure he has his challenges.

As I get down from the tree and look at my monastery a little closer, I begin to realize that you have enlightened me as I continue to search for my identity as you created me. Thank you for letting me find you in your divine providence: in my family with Anne, Tim, and Patty; at work with all the children that you help me take care of; in the parents taking care of their children and helping me, letting them know that they are doing a good job; in the nurses, staff, and my colleagues who, as a team, take care of your most precious ones.

Thank you, Lord, for being with me.

# Chapter 13

# Finding God Again

*August 2009*

The green leaves by our lake cottage now cover all the brown tree branches with different shades of brightness on the surface of the leaves: the darker green leaves embed themselves in the background and middle of the trees, while the bright ones jump out at me as a new day is beginning. The sky is mostly blue with a few clouds scattered around. The dew is still on the grass blades, while the sun is in the process of rising. It is very quiet, aside from the occasional passing car, my feet hitting the pavement, and the breaths I take as I run down the tree-lined road. Despite being mid-July, the air is crisp and not humid. My shirt is soaked from the first four miles of running, and my legs are beginning to tire.

It has been more than two decades since I have gone on a long run out in the country. Dad and I used to run on country roads when I moved back to the United States from Colombia, South America, when I was seventeen years old. It always felt good to leave the busy and noisy world and run for a good hour. We usually chatted about life and the Chicago Bears, and we used our ability to carry on a conversation without effort as a measure of not going too fast with our pace. Although passing cars would sometimes drive faster than the fifty-miles-per-hour speed limit, it was actually the barking dogs dashing into the road that we had to be careful with. In contrast to running in the noisy city, the quietness along the country roads allowed for more introspection.

As I enter the fifth mile, doubt begins to surround me as I wonder if I can finish my six-mile run today. Some information on the dashboard is positive, and some indicates that I am starting to struggle. My pace, albeit slower compared to my midweek runs, seems to be steady, and I am still maintaining a good rhythm with each stride. My legs, however, feel heavy. My heart rate monitor tells me that I am cruising at about 85 percent of my maximum heart rate, letting me know that the tank is starting to get empty. On the other hand, my breathing is comfortable when I take a breath for every two strides. Perhaps there is a sense of comfort in knowing that I can at least get five miles in today.

As I make my final turn on the road and begin to run toward the lake for my last mile, I encounter the wind and find the sun is not shielded anymore, as knee-high corn has replaced the tall trees. The heat has become a heavy load on my shoulders, and the wind has disrupted my rhythm. Even small elevations in the road have become challenging, and now, every step seems to require much effort and mental focus. Once again, I seem to enter a state of prayer as I parallel my run with life. In an introspective and spiritual analysis, I contemplate the challenges in life and how I relate to them, based on my present state of spiritual progress.

There have been times when I have felt God fervently, when not only could I sense God's quiet, persistently strong peacefulness and love in everything I did, but emotionally, I could feel joy. My spiritual state seemed to be in balance, with a constant prayer of meekness and humility, while carrying out God's will of being a servant at home and at work, regardless of the challenges I encountered in life.

Day in and day out, there was a constant rhythm to my stride that did not seem to be disturbed much. Even if my days were incredibly busy and events seemed not to go the way I initially thought they ought to, I still felt connected with God at the end of the day. Being able to say to God at the end of the day, "Thank you for letting me be your helper today, and I hope I did a good job for you," seemed to carry a tremendous amount of peace and satisfaction.

But these states of spiritual connection don't last forever. Sooner or later, I make a turn on the road, where the wind will begin to blow on my face, and I will feel the heat on my shoulders. I don't feel God's joy either in prayer or in daily events, which slowly sends me into a state of complacency in prayer, where I gradually pull away from God. Although I may pray every day, the prayer is a little rushed, or perhaps I don't talk to God throughout the day like I usually do. I gradually let the busyness of life take over the disposition of my heart, so the compass does not point in God's direction all the time. I develop again a sense of independence, and my will becomes strong again. It is in this spiritual state that I begin to make mistakes from being impatient, not showing enough charity, being selfish, not seeing God in every individual, or not being able to feel their love and need. My soul then begins to feel anxious, frustrated that things are not going my way, and disappointed that I have pulled away from God. I then begin to crave getting back to God, to feel God's presence better, but I have to contend with my will that says I'm OK and that I can get by without needing to go to confession. After much internal debate, I finally find peace again by going to reconciliation.

My run today, compared to other runs, where I've had to stop and walk because I was tired, is a little different because I have decided to endure the weather challenges and the tiredness in my legs. Even though I may not feel the joy of running, with the nice, steady rhythm of every stride, I have decided to have faith that I can endure. "Just be with me, God; help me finish."

As I finish the run and I walk afterward to cool down, it hits me that I need to endure better in prayer life so that I don't pull away from God like I have done in the past. While it has been nice that God has touched my soul so that I have felt joy, either in prayer or in life's moments, I need to recognize that I need to endure in prayer, even if God chooses not to touch me or console me. I simply need to have faith that God is with me and that God is happy with my work, and therefore, I need continue to do God's work, regardless of whether or not I get feedback from God or how it affects my emotions.

While my intellect understands that God sometimes withdraws these consolations to help me increase my faith, I can tell it is my heart that needs to understand this concept better. Help me, Lord, so that I may have better faith in you.

This act of discipline has to be one of the tougher acts in following Jesus. Don't we all get worn down by life, with all its busyness to make appointments, meet deadlines, and attend to our obligations and responsibilities? It is during these times that we are more likely not to pray, not to be in touch with God. We feel distant from God as we immerse ourselves in this active life, especially if we don't feel God's touch in our hearts to remind us that God is with us. During these times, when it seems dark outside and we don't see very well with our hearts, we need to believe that it is good to be with God, to make an effort to feel God's love and peace, and to rest in God's arms. Sometimes, God consoles us with this love and peace, but sometimes that does not happen, and we need to know that our prayers reflect our love for God, our dedication, our abiding, our desire to realize that we are dependent on God. This, in turn, makes God very joyous.

As I finish this chapter, I think about persevering in prayer and having better faith in God. Thank you, God, for giving me the discipline to continue to work on prayer, to connect with you, and to be one with you. Thank you, God, for bringing me closer to you and for relieving my anxieties about not praying enough or not well enough. All you care is that I think of you and try to abide by you, just like you abide by me.

# Chapter 14

# Toast and Strawberry Jam

*October 2009*

It is midmorning, and I finally have enough energy to get out of bed and walk down the hall. My legs are weak, and my steps are short. I feel light-headed, and my stomach is somewhat tight, perhaps a little achy. It is no fun being sick with vomiting and diarrhea, and I am thankful that I had a quiet night without further vomiting. My tongue feels dry, and I can tell I carry that smell of illness and sweat; I definitely need a shower.

One of the unfortunate circumstances of having abdominal surgery is the development of scar tissue inside the abdomen, which can bind bowel together. Sometimes this scar tissue can block a bowel and cause an obstruction. The presenting sign of bowel obstruction after somebody has had abdominal surgery is vomiting. I felt insecurity, perhaps some fear, that I might have a bowel obstruction. Memories of being in the hospital with a tube down my nose to the stomach, the pokes to get an IV started, the blood draws—all of those memories went through my head as I threw up the day before. If there was ever a moment to be happy about having some lose stools, this was it—having developed diarrhea this morning meant that I had an infection instead.

"Come along with me," God said as I strolled into the kitchen. After not being able to eat for two days and taking only sips of water and juice early this morning, I am looking forward to putting some solid food in my stomach. As I sit at the table and contemplate the backyard through our dining room window, I appreciate the sun shining on the mix of green, yellow, and orange leaves on the trees and the birds flying from branch to branch. That first bite of toast and strawberry jam brings peace and joy. It settles all anxiety over being hospitalized for dehydration. More important and besides satisfying my hunger, the sweet taste of the jam makes me feel alive again. I can savor it on my tongue and against my palate before I swallow and take another bite. That sweet taste represents that source of energy that will begin my healing as I look forward to a new day.

So goes my life with prayer. I go through periods of time where I believe God consoles me and engulfs me in God's love and then, without being able to anticipate that a change in my relationship with God has taken place, my prayer becomes routine and not affectionate. I let the busyness of life take over my time and ability to communicate with God. I wonder, at times, if I had foreseen the changes, perhaps I could have corrected what I was doing wrong in my prayer and in my time management and therefore maintained that level of affection. Although, even at other times, when it seemed that I had enough time to pray, I must admit I somehow still did not feel the affectionate connection with God. At this point in my mental debate, I realize that I am being selfish for seeking prayer in such a way, seeking to receive consolations and wanting to experience joy for my own benefit.

I then realize that I need to humble myself better and let God direct me in prayer. Most likely, I am going through these periods of roughness because God is trying to work on my humility and meekness. In addition, I think God knows that I need to work on my faith, in that belief that God is always with me and is here to take care of me.

My prayer has evolved through the years. Most recently, I have been doing Sacred Space on the internet through my BlackBerry phone while I eat breakfast in the morning. Sacred Space is a website created by Jesuit priests based in Dublin, Ireland. Small conversations with God through the day lead me to reading about the saints in the evening, which then allows me to contemplate for a bit before bedtime. I have come to appreciate that God doesn't speak to me with words but with movements or feelings in my heart.

Yet despite all these chats with God, I have felt lately that something has been missing in my prayer. As a result, sometimes I feel anxious about wanting to make prayer better, but I am not sure what is needed to make it better. In situations like this, I have come to appreciate that God, somewhere along the way, will show me the path if I am patient enough to wait and let God's divine providence work on me. "Come along with me," God says one more time.

After realizing in July that I needed to be patient and persevere in my prayer, Father Fitz mentioned to me in August that maybe I would like to try doing the Liturgy of the Hours, also known as the Divine Office or the Breviary. Priests use this as part of their praying during the day, but laypeople can learn from this as well. This is a four-volume set with psalms, antiphons, and prayers to help us pray at certain times of the day, including early morning, midmorning, noon, midafternoon, evening, and nighttime. These books look thick, and the pages are thin, like Bible pages. My first reaction was to say no because I did not have enough time in the day to dedicate myself to that much prayer. And then, immediately, I realized, God was talking to me, so how could I possibly turn God down? This was probably the change I was looking for, and God was challenging me to go deeper in prayer. More importantly, God knew this was the direction I was supposed to take, and God, through Father Fitz, knew better than I did. I should respect that.

It took me a little over a week to get into a rhythm of praying with the Liturgy of the Hours, although I was only doing prayer in the morning, noon, and nighttime. These books are filled with the psalms, for which I did not have an appreciation in the past. These prayers felt as if they were written by guys who were whining frequently because somebody was torturing them, or they were in a battle and they were about to lose. I like a couple of psalms because the prayer was about longing for God, but otherwise, I could not relate to them. Now, I found myself praying them as part of my new direction. I felt I had to be patient and persevere in this format of prayer if change was going to take place. What soon followed was a discovery that I never imagined could happen to me. I found joy in praising, honoring, and worshipping God. The psalms were very poetic and carried a rhythm that made my heart want to dance.

This feeling took me back to Colombia when I was a kid. The city of Cali, where I grew up while attending grade school and high school, sits in a valley between two Andes Mountain ranges, or *cordilleras* in Spanish, at about three thousand feet. Sometimes, we would leave the city and drive up into the mountains for a Sunday afternoon visit. The mountains appeared to be very quiet, away from the city noise, and pretty cold. We usually had to bring jackets, whereas we wore T-shirts in the city. The air felt fresh and crisp. We usually ran out in the fields and sometimes would pick fruit from the trees. It felt very free and liberating.

With this memory in place, I felt as if I was in an open field of grass and by mountains with nearby beds of flowers and dandelions. Blackberries and raspberries were hanging from the trees. I could breathe the cool, fresh air while I danced and ran without stopping. By praying these psalms, I felt joy, but it was deeper in my heart; I felt more love and peace.

As I developed a routine of doing the Liturgy of the Hours, I found that my prayer had shifted one more time. Now, I long to praise God throughout the day. I am better able to see God in people, and it has made it easier for me to be God's servant. All I want to do, day in and day out, is to be a good helper to God. It gives me joy to take care of kids in the office and to help at home, whether I am cooking a meal, cleaning house, or helping the kids with their homework. I can feel the joy that Saint Francis and Mother Teresa must have felt by being good servants every day.

Once again, I am thankful to God for helping me be patient and for giving me the ability to persevere. Sometimes this energy comes from deep within the heart, and it appears to be unshakable, where no distraction from life can take me away from this energy.

It is hard to know sometimes how God directs us in life. We often feel like we want to be in control of our lives, and this desire can permeate our prayer lives. We may even get used to a routine and become comfortable with it. It may be difficult to contemplate change, especially if we are not sensitive to what our hearts are telling us—that we need a change. But if we can trust God and ask for guidance in this change, then God, in God's own time, will grant us that favor. And usually, this change moves us closer to God. We just have to be patient and allow God to take control of the wheel.

While I bask in God's consolation—a state of divine healing with peace, love, trust, and serenity—I wonder how long this will last before I encounter another turn or challenge in my prayer. I think of consolations as an intervention by God after some suffering, whether physical, emotional, or spiritual. In particular, they seem to come to me when I feel I have hit bottom, and I cannot make it better by myself. It is in prayer that I find God holding me in quietness, peacefulness, and in love. Then, I can feel the problem or suffering going away, or if it doesn't go away in the form I envisioned, at least God puts things in perspective to make me realize that our love for each other is stronger and more peaceful than the problem itself.

Although I realize I am weak in my faith, I have hope that God will continue to guide me on the right path. For now, thank you, God, for showing us how to pray deeper, to experience better the joy and love you have for each one of us, and for giving us these consolations. Thank you for helping us to be patient and for giving us the insight to allow you to direct us in prayer.

For now, I intend to enjoy this piece of toast and strawberry jam that God has given me today.

# Chapter 15

# Yellow, Orange, Red
# ... and Brown

*October 2010*

The leaves have begun to change color as we head toward Halloween, and the temperature has cooled into the fifties. It is a process that is appealing to the eye and is inviting for family car rides. It is a call of preparation to ready for the winter as we store away furniture, toys, and gardening tools and clean out the garage so we can put the cars away. It is a time to breathe in the fresh air and go out for healthy evening walks.

Yet I wonder how this life change could be felt by the leaves themselves, if they could feel like we do. It is interesting how the change to cooler temperature causes a gradual death. At first, the streets become lined with beautiful hues of orange, yellow, and red. In a few weeks, as the air continues to cool, the leaves turn brown, shrivel up, and then fall to the ground. I wonder if, during the month of August, they feel any anxiety about their impending death as they will stop making chlorophyll in September, which allows them to change color. Or do they feel any pain during the process of changing color and then mourn the loss of their pride as they go from bright tones to brown?

What I find most amazing is that they remain connected to their tree until their time of death. Despite knowing their fate, they humbly and meekly stay attached. They stay attached during this process of changing color. They probably feel a joy in changing from green to yellow or red, just as we appreciate the sunlight piercing those hot colored and iridescent leaves. It is a change that is sweet and painful at the same time, yet they remain loyal to their tree until the end.

I have been challenged with two main events this year. I applied for a high school soccer coach position, and I applied for a new job position but still in the field of pediatrics. I got neither job. I thought I had the qualifications for both jobs, but they didn't work out. The rejections were hard to take, and it was difficult not to take it personally, even though, deep inside, I understood it was about God's divine providence. It seemed as if that beast clothed in pride had popped its head up one more time. How could they have turned me down? This was another challenge in understanding the polarized worlds of pride and humility, of control and meekness.

It is interesting that sometimes we encounter situations in life that seem to have a repetitive theme. They may occur in different circumstances, but they have the same underlying subject. For example, I may have my patience tested at home one day, at work the next day, or in a soccer game on a different day. Worse yet, my patience may be tested in all three environments on the same bad day. For me, it seems like the themes of pride and humility keep coming up every so often.

I have been working on humility over the decades by allowing God to change me. God places me in situations where I realize that God is ultimately the boss, and God calls the shots. These situations usually unfold in a way different from what I initially thought or expected the outcome to be. As a consequence, my prayer also has changed so that even though I may desire to go in a certain direction, I respectfully acknowledge and accept that, ultimately, it is God's will if I go on a different path.

But with these two events this year, God has pushed me to go deeper in my understanding of humility. I really wanted to get those positions, particularly with my credentials, expertise, and accomplishments, but God chose for me to go in a different way. God felt so powerful and so in control. I felt as if I had put my best foot forward, but God had other plans for me. If there was an ounce of pride left in me, and of course there was, I felt like it was completely stripped away from me. In addition, I felt I had lost any sense of control and desire for what I wanted because God was in control. And just like that, when this realization occurred, I felt that a new door had opened, one where I felt in my heart, not just in my mind and intellect, that I was so dependent on God. It didn't matter what gifts or talents I had; God would choose for me. With the opening of this door, I gained more insight into being God's servant.

As I contemplated the change of the leaves and asked God to help me discern the true nature of these events and to help understand my feelings, I came to realize that perhaps it wasn't just humility that was an issue, but maybe I needed to deal with meekness as well. I felt a sense of grief for losing my ability to get what I desired or what I thought God desired for me. I did not have a strong feeling from God that the soccer coach position should be mine. As a consequence, I was not too disappointed when I did not get it. But the feeling was different in the job search, and I thought I had a good chance to change jobs. I was able to envision myself in the new job, so the rejection came a little harder.

In the past, while in the midst of God's presence, I have been able to feel God's desires, and they usually came in strong impulses. In the midst of being silent, I could hear the *bing* with a pure tone and a sweet but short fading echo. This impulse would usually come with a vision or feeling of what was about to happen or should happen. I usually could discern when an impulse was strong and clear enough that I could tell the difference between what God desired for me and when the desire was of my own origin.

For some time, I have given myself more to God and have just wanted to be God's servant, not desiring for myself but simply wanting to listen to God and do God's will. The problem I have encountered recently is that I am not feeling God's desires as I used to do. It's almost as if God has been silent. I have found myself in uncharted territory, as sometimes I felt what I desired, hoping that it was God's desire as well, but then things did not necessarily happen the way I envisioned. I have been having a hard time discerning God's will.

Not getting those two positions turned out to be challenges for me because I thought they were also God's will. I thought these desires came from God. I became confused about what I thought God desired for me. I may have tricked myself or simply have fallen into temptation by pride and control—the feeling that I had the qualifications to make me a good candidate for these positions. I felt a slow burn with both of these events, and I think God reminded me that God needed to continue to work on me, particularly trying to sculpt out these imperfections fueled by pride.

The irony of spiritual development is coming to an understanding, both intellectually and in the heart, that God's healing of my wounds, the healing of these imperfections, are the same wounds inflicted by God's divine providence. In these particular scenarios, I felt that I should have gotten the positions because I had the qualifications for them. It created in me a sense of confidence, perhaps entitlement, that my qualities were good enough for the positions. I could sense that pride was at work here, but God had other ideas about the direction of my life. As it turned out, I stayed with my group and found a renewed love for taking care of the kids in an outpatient setting.

God, who is so loving and infinite, who can embrace me with love and cause a slow and sweet burn in my soul, allows these wounds to take place. These wounds are painful, distressing, anxiety-provoking, and sometimes fearsome. But I seem to be gaining an understanding in my heart of the reason for their occurrences, as I am a sinner with many imperfections. God wants to bring me closer but needs to purify me. As Jesus said in the Sermon on the Mount (Matthew 5:8), "Blessed are the pure in heart, for they will see God."

This understanding, this grace by God, gives me consolation to endure these wounds and to endure the healing of these wounds by God. I can't say that I have reached the level of joy that the saints talk about, where they welcome more situations in which wounds are inflicted upon them. But I can say that I am more accepting of these situations, although somewhat imperfectly, as I have done this year, as I struggle in some situations with anxiety and distress, while, in others, I suffer in peace.

As I thought about and discerned these concepts through the fall season, time has passed, and I have seen all the leaves fall to the ground. The trees are bare, and I now wear my winter coat on walks. My heart remains unsettled, as I feel there is more to these two events than simply looking at humility and meekness, more than looking at how to discern God's desires for me from my own desires. As I dig deeper into my heart, I realize that I am mourning the loss of myself or the image as people see me. It hurts to be rejected. There is a sense that I don't belong. Although I understand intellectually that God cares for me, that God loves me, my heart still seeks the approval, the acceptance, and the love of other people. I struggle letting go of this and simply accepting that God loves me.

More time has passed in November, and I find myself on an afternoon run. The sidewalk is wet, and the leaves are scattered. My gloves give my hands comfort as I run in my favorite navy-blue shorts. As I lose myself in a good rhythm in the fresh, cold air, an image comes to me in which I am standing unclothed in front of God. I know cars are going by, the air is cool on my skin, and sweat is pouring down my forehead. All of these facts give evidence to the reality of the moment. Yet as I am aware that I am running down the street, time and space become still. God looks at me, and I look at God. I feel no attachments to people, places, careers, or emotions. People's perceptions of me, whether positive or negative, do not matter anymore. A sense of peace settles in my heart. As I continue to gaze at God, I feel enveloped by God's love. I then realize that I am God's beloved son, with whom God is well pleased. I simply am, and I belong to God.

Sometimes we get stuck in other people's perceptions of us, and we want approval from them. We want to be accepted as we are and to become part of the team. Sometimes this need to be accepted has nothing to do with our credentials or who we are. Things worked out in the way they did because, perhaps, there were other circumstances beyond our control or somebody else was better qualified. In either case, we feel hurt when we are not chosen; people have not chosen us. We often try to rationalize why we were not chosen, but we still hurt in the depths of our hearts. These events challenge us to look deeper in our hearts, to see who can meet our need of wanting to be accepted, our need to belong, in an unconditional way. This is where God comes in, if we will allow God to gaze at us and appreciate us for who we are and what we are. While resting quietly or maybe during a run, we detach ourselves from the world and feel God's love. Unconditionally!

The clarity of this vision tells me I have returned to my true home. I have found rest in God one more time, and I simply want to be in an embrace with God. It does not matter by whom I am accepted; what matters is that God accepts me for who I am, just as I am. Thank you, Lord, for taking care of me, for inflaming me with your love so that you can help me spread your love.

# Chapter 16

# Warmth in the Middle
# of the Winter

*February 2012*

The swoosh of the skis and snowboards coming down the slopes raised my excitement as I walked to the sitting area behind the main lounge. The crisp evening air in this northern Michigan ski resort breathed energy into what had become difficult and frustrating years. As I looked up, the numerous stars in the dark-blue night embraced me as I took a seat in the twenty-five-degree weather. My new white-and-blue coat gave me warmth and comfort. Soon, I would see my son come down the middle slope, blazing at a very high speed, perfectly in control of his snowboard, as he turned to his right and made his way to the chairlift.

He had finished his first semester of college and was home for Christmas break. I could tell he was happy to be exploring life on his own; learning time management as to when to study, when to eat, and how late to stay up; making decisions on who to hang out with and whether to continue to play tennis at the collegiate level. Yet there seemed to be an undercurrent of anxiety and apprehensiveness in his eyes, as when life is too fast-paced. As he went from his high school years into college life, we found ourselves having difficulty with connecting and talking; thus, the trip to northern Michigan, suggested by Anne, for some bonding time. He had taught me how to snowboard the previous year, and this trip would provide an opportunity for him to be the teacher one more time.

As I watched him come down, time and again, I thought about the slopes and trails we had hit earlier that afternoon. While I played it safe and took the middle of the slopes, I saw him go up steep hills, disappear into wooded areas, and come flying across, ten feet above the ground, into the middle of my path. With a big smile on his face, he would compliment my snowboarding, and we would continue down together to the bottom of the slope.

Tonight, with my thighs and shoulders tired, I wanted only to gaze at him. I wanted to see his gracefulness and freedom, his determination and bravery. He was my boy, and I wanted to enjoy him.

I have felt attached to Saint Joseph lately. In particular, I have been attracted by his humility, his dedication to his holy family, his dedication to work, and the great example he set for his son, Jesus. There is not much in the Bible about Saint Joseph, but a good statement about him comes from the Gospel of Matthew. In the first chapter, he talks about the genealogy of Saint Joseph to eventually describe the birth of Jesus. In Matthew 1:19, he is about to describe Saint Joseph as becoming the husband to Mary and says, "Because Joseph her husband was faithful to the law ..."

There is not much after that, other than Matthew says to us that he was "faithful to the law," a righteous man. The word *righteous* seems so loaded with meaning. I decided to look up the definition in the dictionary[12] and read, "acting in accord with divine or moral law." As I contemplated Saint Joseph and tried to envision what he looked like and how he worked, I could hear the Lord speaking to Moses (Leviticus 19:2), saying, "Be holy, because I, the Lord, your

God, am holy," and Jesus, in his Sermon on the Mount (Matthew 5:48), saying to me, "Be perfect, therefore, as your heavenly Father is perfect." I had been reflecting on my job as a father to my son and thought about mistakes that I might have made in parenting, probably lacking wisdom and not being able to provide good counsel. As I tried to get close to Saint Joseph and Jesus, I could feel the pull to do what was right, what was divine, all the while acknowledging, in humility, that I am prone to mistakes.

I read *St. Joseph and Daily Christian Living* by Francis L. Filas, SJ,[13] and found the book to be logical in its description of Saint Joseph's life, relying mainly on historical data from the Bible to put together a picture of his life. This reading has helped shape my view of him and helped me establish a relationship with Saint Joseph, one in which I could pray to Saint Joseph and ask him to intercede on my behalf before God. I have looked up to him as a role model. I can only imagine how God must have found great favor with Saint Joseph to pick him as the husband of Mary and father to Jesus. I'm going to guess that God must have loved to gaze at Saint Joseph as a beloved son. I have frequently prayed to Saint Joseph to intercede on my behalf before God so that I may be a good father as well.

As I looked at my son coming down the slopes again, I felt an uneasy feeling in my heart that wanted to jump out at him and tell him that I loved him, that I wanted to pass on all my life experiences to him in one second, that I did not want him to feel anxious or to suffer. But the best I could do at that moment was to feel the warmth of my coat, contemplate the stars in the sky, smell the fresh air, and listen to all the snowboarders and skiers coming down the slopes. I needed God to intervene, to rescue us, to help us come together. We had had such a tight relationship when he was a baby and a kid; I just wanted to have that back.

As I continued to watch Tim come down the slopes, time after time, I gradually found God gazing at me, just as he gazed at Saint Joseph. The love that I felt for my son seemed to be the same love I felt from God. And as I said, "This is my boy," I found God saying to me, "This is my beloved son, with whom I am well pleased." It was good for me to hear these words, to console me and give me confidence that despite mistakes I may have made as a father, I am still loved by God. And so, in turn, I found myself imparting this love to my son. I loved him very much, and he needed to hear these words from me, to soothe him, to console him. He is my beloved son, with whom I am well pleased.

The image that came to my mind, as tears flowed down my cheeks, was Rembrandt's painting *The Return of the Prodigal Son*. I had never seen this painting until I read *The Return of the Prodigal Son, A Story of Homecoming*, by Henri Nouwen.[14] A picture of the painting is on the cover of his book. Rembrandt was inspired by the reading in the Gospel of Luke, the longest parable in the Bible, told by Jesus to tax collectors and sinners (Luke 15:1–3, 11–32). In this parable, after the younger of two sons has decided to come back home after squandering all his money, he kneels before his father in full repentance and seeks his mercy. The father is overjoyed that his son has come back and simply holds him. In his book, Henri Nouwen develops all three characters well (the father, the older son, and the younger son), but it is the father who comes to my mind tonight. I simply want to put my arms around my son and hold him.

And so, as the father held his younger son in the parable, as painted by Rembrandt, and the younger son knelt and wanted to be held, I found God holding me as I held my son, but God was holding my son too. And as the three of us held each other, I realized that it was time for the carpenter to step aside and let his son become the teacher. It was time for me to step aside and let him flourish in his young-adult years to become the person whom God had created him to be. I needed to trust that, in God's divine providence, my son would discover what his college major was going to be, how he was going get internships and experiences to make his résumé strong, how he would handle more responsibilities at home, and how he could show me life from a millennial point of view. Learning how to snowboard was just the beginning of our new relationship. I was going to let him teach me about life and, in the process, hopefully, he would find his true identity as God made him out to be.

A big challenge that all of us parents face as we raise our children is to let them move from their kid years, when we frequently tell them what to do, to their adolescent and young-adult years, when they make heavier decisions on their own. We love our children very much, with all our hearts, and we want nothing more than to see them come out ahead and to do well. When we intervene during their adolescence and young adulthood, we do so with the hope that they won't fall. After all—and rightly so—they have decided to take the reins and to command their own lives. We are afraid that they will fall and make mistakes. Yet this is vital to their development, as long as they remain in a circle of safety. When we become comfortable with allowing them to make mistakes, and we give them advice in a nonjudgmental way, then we also have grown as parents.

Thank you, God, for showing us your love, for embracing us and making us feel that we belong to you. Thank you for helping me find my identity as a father, as you are a Father to me, and hopefully helping my son to find his identity, as you made him out to be. In the middle of this cold weather in northern Michigan, you have flamed our hearts with your love and have helped the three of us to be one.

# Chapter 17

# I in You, and You in Me

*October 2012*

Anne was attending an educational conference, and I decided to tag along to get away, relax, exercise, and do some reading. We were supposed to stay at the main conference center in a one-bedroom suite, but we got moved to a six-bedroom house at the golf and ski resort. The house was well kept, clean, modern-looking, and very large. This was an unexpected surprise, as all the rooms were already taken at the main conference center. I felt some guilt, staying in such a large place at the cost of a much smaller suite, but the location by the eighteenth hole provided an environment for much prayer and meditation.

The previous week had been difficult while I pondered the possibility that I might have multiple myeloma. An elevated total protein on a routine chemistry profile prompted my primary care physician to order additional tests, including what turned out to be a mildly elevated monoclonal antibody level. Although I did not have any symptoms to go along with the diagnosis, I nevertheless began to deal with the concept that multiple myeloma is rarely cured.

Multiple myeloma is a cancer of the plasma cells, which are white blood cells that have become specialized in producing specific types of antibodies to specific diseases. For example, after we encounter a bout with the chicken pox virus, our white cells will be involved in a fight to kill the virus. After the war is over, some of the white cells will become plasma cells and will serve as memory cells for the next time we encounter the chicken pox virus. If some plasma cells decide to go rogue, produce an antibody that is not normal, and reproduce out of control, then we have the potential to develop multiple myeloma, a cancer that spreads into the bone marrow and then damages bones, the immune system, and kidneys. My current condition has been diagnosed as MGUS (monoclonal gammopathy of undetermined significance), where I have an elevation of this abnormal antibody but don't have symptoms or signs of multiple myeloma yet.

After so many years of dealing with testicular cancer, which continued to remain in remission after my last relapse in 2000, I now began to deal with the possibility of having another type of cancer. It is my understanding that the possibility of developing multiple myeloma is not related to having had chemotherapy for the testicular cancer. Some might consider this bad luck, but I have come to appreciate that these obstacles are for my benefit as I try to get closer to God.

As I had in the past, I had to deal with my own mortality and worry for my family. Would they be OK without me? Would it matter if I was gone? Could they adjust if I was gone? How impressionable would my death be on my nineteen-year-old son and fifteen-year-old daughter? God had given me the grace to understand, when I had my last relapse for testicular cancer in 2000, that they would be fine if I were to die. This provided much relief and freedom to reach a better connection with God, to have better faith, and to love God more freely without attachments. But I found myself struggling with this again. I tried to go back to that moment when God bathed me with God's grace, but I couldn't grab it. I knew it had to come from God, but it wasn't coming to me. I pleaded with God to have mercy on me and to help me deal appropriately with this challenge. I wasn't sure of the purpose of this obstacle, but at a minimum, I knew I needed to go deeper with my faith in God.

If I was going to develop further my relationship with God, I needed to experience the freedom to follow God. And to do this, I needed to put behind me the past memories of God touching me and giving me assurance that I would be fine and that my family would be fine. I needed to go down the path with God and not feel any attachments to the past but to experience God in the present. Only then would I be able to feel God's love and experience the freedom to accept it. If I believed this to be true, then God would take me by the hand, lead me, and walk with me. If God gave me the grace to experience this freedom and if I was humble enough to accept this walk, then God would bathe me in God's love.

The next day, after checking in and after Anne went to her conference, I sat on the deck by the family room, overlooking the eighteenth hole and listening to Native American flute music from my iPhone. The gentle wind blew through the leaves, and the breeze turned cool later in the afternoon. I soon had to wear my sweatshirt, despite the clear sunny skies. It was late August in upper Michigan, and it felt like the fall season was upon us. My gaze became fixed on the trees, and I appreciated the mixture of shaded and bright-green leaves. The wind blew them in undulating waves, as if they sang a song of comfort to my heart, and soon, I found myself in deep communion with God.

I began to praise God for being such a good Father and for taking such good care of us. I felt our Blessed Mother and Saint Joseph were there with me. I thanked them for being there with me. I prayed to Saint Francis to help me to be a good servant. All I wanted to do was to take good care of children, help them get better, and be a good father and a good husband. I felt joy to be a servant for God, all for God's glory. I prayed for my grandparents who had passed. I could feel Grandma Murphy there with me. I also prayed for my father-in-law; for my uncles, aunts, and cousins; and for patients who had also passed away. I prayed for our friend Annette and her dad; I prayed for their peace and for their communion with God.

Very slowly, my mind began to shut down. I became engulfed in the rhythm of the leaves moving back and forth. I then became thoughtless. I was just being, just resting in God—and then a joy, peace, and love overcame me. I felt a poem burst out of me:

> Your arms engulf me,
> Your touch is delicate.
> Not by the fire that purifies my soul,
> But by your warmth, Father,
> I realize you are here to console me.
> My heart is at peace,
> Weightless and without care,
> For there are no regrets from yesterday,
> Nor worries about tomorrow,
> But simply joy in being here with you,
> Joy to be here with my brothers and sisters.
> As I rest in you
> I feel complete.
> I am in you,
> And you are in me.

As I rested in God's arms, I felt as if Jesus was with me, doing his high-priestly prayer to God the Father (John 17:1–26). In the middle of his prayer, I heard Jesus say,

> My prayer is not for them alone. I pray also for those
> who will believe in me through their message, that
> all of them may be one, Father, just as you are in me
> and I am in you. May they also be in us so that the
> world may believe that you have sent me. I have given
> them the glory that you gave me, that they may be

one as we are one—I in them and you in me—so
that they may be brought to complete unity. Then
the world will know that you sent me and have loved
them, even as you have loved me. (John 17:20–23)

The Father, the Son, and the Holy Spirit of love, all in one, as
we rested together.

I rested in God's arms for some time, feeling love and peace and
unaware of time passing by. But then my mind wanted to get busy:

In dismay, perhaps disbelief, I asked God, "Why are you treating
me this way? Why are you doing this to me?" I felt overwhelmed by
this feeling. I was engulfed in this love and wanted to wiggle out.

"I don't deserve to be treated this way, Lord. I am a sinner with
much fault, and you are loving me beyond my understanding." I
did not know how to act. I wanted to move. I wanted my mind to
become active, but I felt God tell me to just rest. *"Don't let your mind
get busy"* is how I felt. And so, I rested in God again. I let go of my
impulse to move away and went back to letting God hold me.

I don't know how long the moment lasted, but an image then
came into my mind, which was actually a memory from when I was
a child. I had been playing outside all day with my friends, and it
was now evening. My mom called me to come home, and my first
reaction was of disappointment and perhaps some resistance to come
home. But I obeyed, and once inside, I felt the warmth of being
home, with all the security and love that made me feel better.

After a brief pause, my mind became busy again, trying to sort
out what had just happened. I felt overwhelmed by my connection
with God but also wondered what God was trying to tell me with
that memory. It was too much to digest that evening, and I had to
let the moments be for what they were and not try to tamper with
or distort them.

I don't know what is going to happen with this diagnosis of
MGUS and whether I will progress to multiple myeloma. I don't
know if God is telling me to come home and I'll be OK; that my

family will be OK. At a minimum, God has tugged at me a little more, and I have drawn closer to God a little more.

Sometimes in prayer, we want to direct our wishes and desires in such a way that we want God to answer us and address our needs. Don't we feel impatient like this at times? We hope there is a direct relationship between the expression of our need and the answer we get from God. But God answers us in an unpredictable way sometimes. Interestingly enough, we can hear God's answer if we submit ourselves in humility and in quietness. It may not necessarily address our specific question, but God lets us know that God is with us, caring for us, loving us, and supporting us. And as Jesus says to us, "Surely, I am with you always, to the very end of the age" (Matthew 28:20).

I do believe that God has brought me closer to God out of God's own will, and I could not have done this myself, out of my own will or power. In prayer, I came to realize that I needed to go beyond my memories of God taking care of me in the past and just open myself up to God's touch in the present moment, in humility and with the freedom to accept God's touch. I find myself in a very humble position in accepting this love from God and realizing that I am not much without God.

Thank you, Lord, for taking such good care of me. Thank you for showering me with your love as you came to visit me with the saints, my relatives, and Grandma Murphy. Thank you for showing me the importance of freedom in prayer and not having any attachments to the past or to forms of prayer but simply being there with you and letting you take me by the hand to lead me to peace and love.

# Chapter 18

# Lead Us Not into Temptation

*November 2014*

My monoclonal antibody has gradually risen over the past two years but not significantly enough to put me in the range of a multiple myeloma diagnosis. I have remained healthy while the testicular cancer tumor markers remain in the normal range. As I headed into 2014, I found myself, one more time, being challenged with the political aspect of practicing medicine.

It was early spring 2014, and there was still some snow on the front lawns. The air felt frigid, and I needed a walk. My heart felt restless with some confusion: disappointed, perhaps some anger, isolated. As I walked down the sidewalk, the beginning of Mel Gibson's *The Passion of the Christ*[15] came into my view. I could visualize the beginning of the movie: It was dusk, and the fog was heavy on the ground. Jesus's heavy garments provided some comfort from the cool temperatures. The olive trees were bare, and not an animal was in sight. He looked at the sky, as if petitioning God, and then he fell on his knees. His face was weary and in pain. As he foretold the night before, he seemed to be concerned that he was about to be betrayed. But he felt a heavier burden: he was about to carry with him all the sins of this world. He was the promise that we could conquer death. He was our Messiah. But in his humanity, he realized this burden was heavy—very heavy.

"Hear me, Father, rise up and defend me. Save me from the traps they set for me," Jesus prayed.

"Do you really believe that one man can bear the full burden of sin?" asked the devil as he paced slowly around the Lord, as if waiting for the opportune time to seize him.

"Shelter me, oh Lord. I trust in you. In you, I take refuge."

"No one man can carry this burden, I tell you. It is far too heavy. Saving their souls is too costly. No one. Ever. No. Never."

"Father, you can do all things. If it's possible, let this chalice pass from me, but let your will be done, not mine."

As Jesus fell to the ground, the devil looked at him with a smile, as if he had conquered him. His eyes were focused on Jesus, and he enjoyed the moment of seeing Jesus down. A serpent moved from underneath the devil's cloak and headed toward Jesus. Jesus continued to suffer, while Peter, James, and John were asleep. He felt our despair, our detachment from God, and every one of our sins. But his expression changed. By the grace of God, his fortitude and magnanimity reawakened. Jesus gradually rose to his feet. Feeling exhausted and sweating profusely, he turned and looked back at the guards coming to get him. This was the moment he had anticipated. He knew he was going to be handed over. This was the turning point when the fight would begin. With meekness and humility, he would conquer death. He would do it for us. With strong and simple determination, he stepped on the serpent, and the devil disappeared.

I saw Jesus being tempted by the devil, and Jesus, in his humanity, prayed to God to let this chalice pass him by. He experienced weaknesses, just like I did. He suffered, just like I did. But Jesus is also God, so he was able to conquer the devil. I have been feeling that I could make my problem better by myself, neglecting to admit that I needed God to help me deal with it, to make it go away. Instead, lately, I have been feeling like the devil has been prowling around me, saying, "Do you believe that you can bear the burden of sin? No one can carry this burden—no one, never."

I was asked to step down as the leader in our pediatric group. My feelings at the time were mixed, as I acknowledged my tiredness from serving in this role for three and a half years. Our group has leadership terms of two years, and I was serving my second term. We had already elected our new leader, who was to take over at the end of the year, but I was asked to step down early. There was a sense of relief in letting somebody else step up. I was tired of the role and the responsibility, but I was stepping down in a negative light. I was not performing to their liking. I wanted to be humble and be positive, but my heart was groaning in pain. My mind was busy as I analyzed the mistakes that I may have made and how I could have done a better job. I had a hard time letting go. I simply wanted to do a good job, but it was hard to acknowledge that, in some way, I had failed the organization. I came to believe that if I analyzed the situation enough, I could learn from it and make things better. And just like that, I fell into the temptation of self-sufficiency, thinking I could make things better by myself.

I remembered when I first took the leadership role. I prayed to God to guide me, to help me be humble, and to have the Holy Spirit illuminate me. And although I had a sense that the responsibility would be for a short time—it was supposed to be just two years—I somehow forgot that in my heart. I slowly became engulfed in the responsibilities of being a leader. Weeks turned into months, which then became years. I became attached to the role.

Now, months later after I was asked to step down, I found myself in a state of self-healing; I wanted some peace. As time passed, I came to realize that I was not making progress in finding peace in my heart. There was a pain that was masked by the pride of a good appearance on the outside, while being in a negative light. Not that I desired to be in a negative light, but I was concerned with outward appearance. I thought I could change that outward appearance by myself, if that was important enough to me. I thought that changing that outward appearance would bring peace to my heart.

I soon realized that the outward appearance was not the important issue. This was not a new revelation to me, for I knew that outward appearances were not important, but I just didn't feel the change in my heart. My heart was craving acceptance. Instead of thinking how to make things better from the outside, I needed to go deeper in my restless heart to find peace. I soul-searched but could not find the solution. Once again, I found myself trying to solve the problem by myself and not letting God into my heart to help me see better. Once again, pride was at work in my heart and leading me into self-sufficiency.

As the flowers began to bloom and the grass turned kelly green, my vision pointed toward God. I knew that I needed to humble myself before God if I wanted to have God heal me. But humbling myself before God meant giving up control—the control to heal my soul by myself. I had to give up my will and allow God's love to heal me. I felt vulnerable with letting my guard down and letting God heal me, but I nevertheless embraced the concept to let God heal me.

Another month went by, and I continued to struggle. Despite desiring this healing from God as I prayed in my head, it was not happening in my heart. I felt like my prayer was coming up empty. My intellect desired the healing from God, but I was not able to empty myself in my heart. I somehow could not find that ability to create space for God to dwell in my heart.

"I love you, Lord, and I so want to be with you. I want to be one with you. I need your help in my healing," I prayed.

With time and prayer, I could tell that change began to take place in my heart as I was able to humble myself enough to let God do the healing in God's own time. It almost felt like a resignation to let God do God's job, but it felt hopeful. I felt that healing was going to occur, but I wasn't sure when.

Oddly enough, despite the change in my heart, time continued to pass, and spring turned into summer. I tried to be patient, but I anxiously waited for God to touch my heart. Then, one afternoon in July, after a six-mile run, I sat in the backyard to recover and pray. It was a sunny afternoon, and Anne's garden seemed to be full of life. As I thought about God and prayed a little, Psalm 13 came into my heart:

> How long, Lord? Will you forget me forever?
> How long will you hide your face from me?
> How long must I wrestle with my thoughts
> and day after day have sorrow in my heart?
> How long will my enemy triumph over me?
>
> Look on me and answer, Lord my God.
> Give light to my eyes, or I will sleep in death,
> and my enemy will say, "I have overcome him,"
> and my foes will rejoice when I fall.
>
> But I trust in your unfailing love;
> my heart rejoices in your salvation.
> I will sing the Lord's praise,
> for he has been good to me.

As I looked at the red, yellow, and orange flowers that Anne had planted in the spring and the green grass that blanketed the backyard on this unseasonably cool day in July, I felt Jesus step in. To paraphrase Matthew 11:28–29, Jesus said, "Come to me, John, you who labor and are burdened, and I will give you rest. Take my yoke upon you and learn from me, for I am meek and humble of heart."

I held my breath—it was difficult to breathe—and my eyes began to water as I placed his yoke upon me. It seemed to fit me well as I stood next to him. We looked at each other, and he smiled at me. His brown eyes radiated love into my heart, and I felt consoled. He felt like my buddy, like my dear friend. I lowered my guard and let myself become vulnerable as we began to walk together. My burden was lifted, and it no longer mattered how I had performed in my job as a leader, whether I had made good decisions and had good outcomes or had made bad decisions and subsequently had bad outcomes. It did not matter if the organization approved or disapproved of me. At that moment, being with Jesus, as we walked together, brought love and peace. It brought total acceptance by Jesus and by God in total union with the Holy Spirit. I simply rested in contemplation, basking in the warmth of the sun.

Summer turned into fall, and I seemed to have caught a wave of peacefulness, love, and acceptance for quite some time. This theme of pride and humility seemed to be a recurring one, but I felt a deeper sense of humility. I had a deeper appreciation that I was nothing, and I could accomplish nothing without God. I was no more important than anybody out there. And when I looked at people, I saw them as my brothers and sisters, whom God loved very much. God wanted nothing more than their well-being and to have them love God back. I was at the bottom of the pole, as God's messenger and doing God's work; taking care of babies, children, teens, and young adults; and fulfilling my job in my family as a husband and father. But most important, I felt accepted by Jesus and by God, and this acceptance filled my cup, so I did not feel the need to be accepted by others.

As I worked on this chapter and tried to finish some editing, I thought of our Lord's Prayer: "And lead us not into temptation but deliver us from evil." This is such a paradox to me in that I do not want to be tempted because I am a weak creature with many imperfections. It doesn't take much to tip me over. Yet it is in temptation by evil forces that I get to see my shortcomings, which can be healed by God's grace if I'm willing to let God heal me. I need to be humble to recognize this and to allow God to help me.

"Protect me, O Lord, for I do not wish to hurt you," I prayed. I am frequently tempted to be self-sufficient, and this is fueled by pride. This self-sufficiency, in turn, makes it easier for me to fall when I am tempted. "Please don't leave me alone, Lord," I supplicated one more time.

It is through temptation that I see my weaknesses, which allows me to ask for forgiveness when I fall and to seek God's mercy and draw closer to God. This cycle of falling, forgiveness, and mercy pushes me to be more humble as I recognize my dependency on God. It is only in humility that I can bring my will in line with God's will; that I can give up my self-sufficiency and let God flow through me.

As I prayed about all this, I found myself in the Sea of Galilee in Peter's boat with the rest of the disciples (Matthew 14:22–33). Jesus had just passed us, and the disciples thought they had seen a ghost. Jesus asked Peter to walk on the water toward him. I too decided to walk on the water toward Jesus, but I wanted to put my self-sufficiency aside and not be distracted or be tempted to rely on myself as I walked toward Jesus. He stretched out his hand toward me without saying a single word, and, with his brown eyes full of love and deeply looking into my soul, his facial expression asked me to walk toward him, to trust him. And so I prayed, "Help me, oh Lord, to trust in you and to have faith in you. Help me to walk on water toward you."

I think self-sufficiency is one of our strengths that helps us accomplish many things, but it can also become a weakness, in particular as it relates to spiritual development. In the active life, we encounter obstacles on a daily basis, where we learn that sometimes we succeed and sometimes we fail. We prefer to succeed but understand sometimes if we fail, but these events can act as homework as they relate to our relationship with God. At what point do we acknowledge, especially if the endeavor is for a higher good, that perhaps we cannot accomplish a task, and we need God's help or maybe illumination from the Holy Spirit? We get to practice this exercise on a daily basis until we get it right, acknowledging that we need help from God and accepting God's help in God's way or in God's divine providence.

This self-sufficiency is not listed as a sin in the Ten Commandments, but it feels to me like it is right up there as we try to get closer to God. Self-sufficiency, usually fueled by pride, keeps us distant from God.

As I finish this chapter, I thank you, God, for helping me see that I am totally dependent on you. You have enlightened me to see the self-sufficiency that can spring from my heart and my will. By moving this aside, I have allowed your will and love to reign in my heart. You help me overcome my self-sufficiency and help me bring whatever talents I have to the table, place them in front of you, and let you take care of your loved ones through me. Thank you for giving me the strength to endure in prayer and have the patience to wait for your response and healing. Thank you, Jesus, for being with me, for praying for me, and for interceding for me. In your name, I pray.

# Chapter 19

# Lord, Let Me Eat the Crumbs from the Master's Table

*May 2016*

In the beginning was the Word,
and the Word was with God,
and the Word was God.
—John 1:1

The drive to Coldwater, Michigan, was at the beginning of winter. There was snow on the ground, although the highways were clear. The gray skies were in contrast with how our hearts felt—full of anticipation, perhaps some anxiety, maybe some guarded joy, definitely colorful. Christmas Day was four days away, and we were about to bring home the newest members of the family.

Henry and Margaret were ten-week-old English setters, weighing roughly about eight to ten pounds. They had cute round facial features with long black-and-white ears. Their fur was soft, and they were fun to pet, but they were hard to hold because they were so full of energy and wanted to climb up our chests and to our shoulders. They seem to be mostly white with some black ticking. Margaret had a half-black facial mask, whereas Henry had a full black facial mask. After a short visit with the breeders, we were on our way home, with the dogs in one big kennel.

The cold air came in January, along with several feet of snow. For dogs that were only about one foot tall, they did not seem to care that the snow was higher than them. They jumped into it and ran around, creating their own tracks and paths, which they frequented every time they had to go potty. Brother and sister rivalry was in full display as they bit each other's ears, lips, legs, tails, and necks. It didn't matter if they were inside in a warm temperature or outside at twenty degrees. And as quickly as they went out to play and entered full combat against each other, they would tire out and take baby naps.

By February, fun and excitement were gradually replaced by my physical tiredness and stress from work. I began to crave time alone, even small amounts of time, just to pray, but this was hard to come by. I also was working on lectures for our third-year medical students, who were going to start their clinical rotations in May. I found myself getting impatient at times and sometimes experiencing dissatisfaction with life, as I couldn't even get the lectures done. Life became mundane and routine: waking up around 5:00 a.m. to take care of the puppies, snow-blowing or shoveling snow before going to work, taking care of ill patients during the day, sometimes shoveling snow or snow-blowing again after work, taking care of the puppies in the evening, and then getting ready for bed by ten o'clock, before the day would start all over again at five the next morning—and I was not always guaranteed a full night's sleep if the puppies woke up in the middle of the night. Being challenged physically, emotionally, and spiritually, I found myself getting short on patience and not being charitable, not just with Henry and Margaret but also at home. I did a good job at work, maybe a so-so job at home, and certainly didn't feel any love for the puppies. I felt guilty that I could not extend my love to Henry and Margaret, even to the point that I questioned the reason for them being at home. Deep down, I knew this was not right and thought I should be able to extend my love, even to the puppies, but I seemed to not want to give them any importance. I began to pray to God to help me overcome this obstacle, to help me be more charitable and loving, but I was stuck and did not want to let go of that sorry feeling of being tired, physically and emotionally. I wanted to be paid back with rest and with alone time and to be restored back to full strength. As usual, God let me stay in this state for a number of weeks before coming to my rescue.

It was the end of February, and I woke up to Henry's whining. It was 5:15 a.m., and all was dark in the house. I made my way down the stairs to get their collars, grumbling in my heart about why I had to do this and lamenting that I could not sleep longer. As I knelt to Henry's crate and opened the door, he pushed through and into my chest as I put his collar around him, wagging his tail and licking me. I then found myself going into prayer.

I was near Tyre and Sidon in the middle of the day. The sun was bearing down on the dirt roads, people were staying in the shade by trees or their houses, and the chickens were picking at the ground, looking for food. Jesus and his disciples had withdrawn to this area after rebuking the Pharisees for clinging to their traditions and elevating these above mercy and love. Confrontations were becoming more frequent for Jesus, but the time for his crucifixion was not to take place yet, so he needed to withdraw from Israel to this Gentile land. It is hard to know exactly how much time passed, but we know from the Gospel of Saint Matthew that the encounter with the Canaanite woman was in chapter 15 and the Last Supper was in chapter 26.

Tyre and Sidon were two Phoenician cities along the coast of the Mediterranean and still are present today in modern-day Lebanon. Tyre is about twenty miles south of Sidon and about twelve miles from the current-day Israel and Lebanon border.[16] This area was known as the Land of Canaan and was dominant up to approximately 1250–1150 BC, when it is believed a major catastrophe took place, possibly military, that resulted in the dissolution of their land and culture. The Bible has this time in history as the invasion by Hebrew general Joshua and the Israelites.[17] Tyre and Sidon prospered because of their seaports and trade centers. The Canaanites were polytheistic and were considered corrupt and pagan by Israelite standards, a threat to Israel's monotheistic religion and relationship with God. With time, the Canaanites military weakened and became inferior to the Israelites.

With this backdrop, I saw the Canaanite woman approach Jesus (Matthew 15:21–28), crying out to him, "Lord, Son of David, have mercy on me! My daughter is demon-possessed and suffering terribly." Mark also recounts this story and places Jesus in a house where he had chosen to have his disciples rest (Mark 7:24–30). The woman is well aware of the rivalry between the Jews and the Canaanites. She acknowledges Jesus's superior standing as a Jew but also is willing to acknowledge him as the Messiah, since she called him the "Son of David." Jesus does not address her initially, and only after the disciples urge him to send her away does he reply, "I was sent only to the lost sheep of Israel."

The woman, after initially crying out to Jesus for mercy, knelt near Jesus and said, "Lord, help me!"

He replied, "It is not right to take the children's bread and toss it to the dogs."

But in her inferiority and humility, she had acquiesced to the role of a dog while acknowledging Jesus as her master. "Yes, it is, Lord," she said. "Even the dogs eat the crumbs that fall from their master's table." Because of her faith, Jesus healed her daughter.

While I was holding Henry on my chest and then proceeded to get Margaret's collar on, I acknowledged that the winter had become long and difficult. It had become difficult trying to be loving and charitable on my own terms, forcing this desire, while at the same time having the desire to have my own "me time." I acknowledged that I had not let God in to help me with this dilemma because I wanted to do it on my own terms. The load became heavy enough that I finally found myself praying to God, "Lord, have mercy on me. I am one of the dogs right now, and I could eat whatever crumb you let fall from your table."

At that moment, I felt like humility settled in, and I was now ready to accept God's healing. As we went down the sidewalk, with snowbanks on either side, I contemplated the dark, cloudless sky, full of stars. I was in awe that the universe could be so big and so beautiful, and God had created this. In that silent walk, I felt so engulfed by God. My heart felt warm, even though it was fifteen degrees, and steam was coming from my breath. As the dogs searched for a spot to potty on the snow, I continued to feel God in that beautiful sky and let myself drift into the vast space of the universe. Peace settled into my heart, and for that brief moment, as Margaret and Henry locked their eyes on me and I looked at them, I experienced a deep sense of love from them, and, in return, I felt love for them too. We stood looking at each other for what seemed to be minutes but probably was just a few seconds. The cold air began to seep through my coat, and we had to make it back into the house. It was an intense moment, a moment that I was able to bask in that morning, but I forgot the moment in its intensity once I got busy again with life's routines and schedules.

As I went through March, I lost that moment of peace and love in my heart. My memory told it had happened, but I could not feel it again in my heart. It reminded me of Peter trying to build three tents for Jesus, Moses, and Elijah, when Jesus underwent the transfiguration (Matthew 17). The moment was so intense, so full of love and peace, that he wanted to keep it for himself by building those three tents while they were up on the mountain, but Jesus did not want him to freeze-frame it.

As I thought of Peter, I came to realize that Jesus wanted me to understand that these experiences were eternal, without a beginning or an end, and although I wanted to keep it for myself, my faculties would not allow me to remember the intensity of it. I have come to believe that this moment was an infusion of love by God.

It was finally during my stay-home vacation in April, when I had a chance to rest up, that I reflected on the past winter season and, in particular, that magical morning in February. My relationship with the dogs had certainly improved since February, but there was more to this life experience that I did not appreciate back then. At the heart of the matter was my inability to give love and charity while tired, physically, emotionally and spiritually. I clung to the idea that I needed, perhaps deserved, time for myself, an opportunity to rest up. The more tired I felt, the harder I grabbed that concept. Because of this attachment, I lost the freedom to follow God and to let God work through me.

In the theology of Saint John of the Cross, I needed to die more to myself. I frequently thought of him during the winter, as I had so many times before, and I prayed to him to intercede on my behalf as I tried to move closer to God. But the times when I felt him during this past winter season provoked in me a sense of stubbornness. I seemed to be in conflict, where I wanted to endure the tiredness and to work out being more charitable on my own terms, thus letting pride pop up as it had so many times before. But I also wanted a break from the winter challenges. I did not want to die to myself, and I wanted my free time. I wanted to rest, and I did not want to suffer. I think Saint Ignatius of Loyola came to my rescue, as I was able to put in perspective praying for freedom while following his style of prayer. In the Ignatian form of prayer, we begin by being aware of the presence of God; we then pray for freedom to put ourselves at God's disposal; and finally, we do a review of consciousness as we examine the details of our day before we read the gospel for that day and meditate on it. I was able to meditate better on the freedom section and not let myself get anchored with attachments.

This brought back memories of living in Colombia when I was in my teens, and we frequented the River Melendez near Cali. El Rio

Cauca is a large and forceful river, stretching about seven hundred miles from south to north as it goes along the western and central mountain ranges (cordilleras) of the Andes Mountains, before it dumps into the Atlantic Ocean. Tributaries contribute to El Rio Cauca along the city of Cali, including the River Melendez. These tributaries are smaller in width, making them easier to visit. We never said we were going to the River Cauca; it almost implied being crazy, knowing the river was so forceful and the currents so strong. We simply said we were going to the "river," to imply we were going to one of the tributaries.

We loved going there for camping, after playing soccer matches, and after roller-hockey workouts. Although we went to one of its tributaries for safety reasons, that part of the river still seemed wide in some parts, sometimes 150 feet wide. The river had a strong current and could hit the rocks hard, turning the undulating water into white foam and waterfalls. Letting our legs soak in that cool water was a joy. Better yet, letting ourselves float downstream, as we avoided tree branches hanging over the edges of the river and the large rocks in the middle of the river, was a joy. Going down the river, floating in a sitting position with my legs sticking forward to protect against any rocks or tree branches, I could feel the current tilt me to the right and then to the left, sometimes pushing me forward and sometimes slowing me down. The to-and-fro, side-to-side motion seemed so unpredictable, yet soothing in its forceful unpredictability. I loved being weightless in the river.

As I rested on vacation during the month of April, I wanted to flow down the river with its undulating waves. I passed by rocks and sticks and let the current carry me with such force and determination that it knew where it would lead me, to be right there with God. It was in the midst of this current during the month of April, after passing by all those obstacles and stresses from work, the Michigan snow, and the care of the puppies, that I then felt more charity, more love, and more peace in my heart. To paraphrase Saint John of the Cross in his poem "The Living Flame of God," it was as if the veil had been lifted, and I could see more clearly how to be a better servant of God.

I have been letting God guide me in the past decade or so on how to be more humble and meek, as I have acknowledged how pride has gotten in the way of my relationship with God, with Anne, and with taking care of patients and their parents at the office. But with this winter, I think the Holy Spirit wanted to show me the freedom to follow God and to experience better the freedom to serve. This freedom means not having any attachments to this world, whether physical or emotional. Saint John of the Cross goes one step further and includes spiritual attachments, but I'm still working on this one, trying to comprehend in my heart what that means. Freedom also entails giving myself completely into God's hands, with complete trust and faith that God knows what to do with me. It is risky and scary because I cannot see the future, but with God's grace and with the direction of the Holy Spirit, I can have a better hope.

My lesson with this experience was to be able to follow God's lead; to express love and charity, regardless of how tired I felt; and not to be attached to what I thought were my needs—my need to rest and have quiet time. Interestingly enough, this freedom to love the puppies has spilled over into improving my relationship with Anne and taking better care of the children in the office. A deeper sense of peace and love has developed while I try to abide by God, not just in situations when I feel tired but also when these situations are stressful. I am quite sure that I will have more exercises in the future, where I will be challenged to practice this freedom to follow God. In the meantime, I continue to pray in communion with all the saints.

Blessed Mother, you are such a loving mother. Thank you for praying for me. Blessed Saint Joseph, thank you for helping me be a better spouse, father, and physician. Saint John of the Cross and Saint Ignatius, thank you for interceding on my behalf. Holy Spirit, how can I express my gratitude for showing me the freedom to follow God and for allowing me to experience the freedom to receive God's love and to pass it on? You let me discern this topic back in January 2008 (chapter 10) through Father Fitz, and I feel I have a better understanding of experiencing freedom so that I may follow your lead better. Lord Jesus, thank you for bringing yourself to me in the Word, just as you did in Tyre and Sidon. I thank you for taking my load and letting me follow you, and thank you for helping me love better both Margaret and Henry. Amen.

PS: August 2016. As I put the last touches on and do some final editing to this story, I find myself, one more time, being humbled before our Lord. I am like Peter when I say I will not deny you. I will be with you and follow your teachings. But then I deny Jesus, just like Peter did.

Doesn't it seem like sometimes this is the story of our lives? We discern and learn from God, perhaps from going to mass or service or perhaps from a life event that takes place over several months. And then, in an instant, we react from our hearts in a way that our intellect thought should have been better, more kind, more loving. We go through our lives, trying to learn from God and from Jesus, but sometimes the change in our hearts takes a little longer, mostly because our will and pride get in the way. Our hearts think they know better and push God aside.

I have found myself being short again in giving love and charity, as Jesus would give to others. All I can do is bow my head and ask God to take me and accept me as I am, in my full humanity, as I am so prone to making mistakes. But my waiting is not long before God engulfs me in God's arms and says to me one more time, "John, you are my beloved son," and then I feel peace and love again. God understands our humanity and our tendency to make mistakes, and if we are willing, we can let God embrace us and tell us that we are loved, just as we are. Then we can rest.

# Chapter 20

# I Love You More Than These

*July 2018*

The drive to work engulfed me in a beautiful blue sky, not a single cloud in sight. This peaceful moment gave me an opportunity to reflect on my aging process, as I felt the stiffness and mild swelling in my left knee. Even the daily low-back pain with tingling in my left foot was present. At times, I have a hard time believing that I am aging as I turn fifty-seven years old and entertain memories from my youth, particularly as they relate to soccer. I was off from playing soccer for a few years, having decided to focus on my running for some time, and now I'm back to playing soccer again.

Last night's game was not a good performance. I have been playing in a drop-in over-thirty league with guys who are skilled. Some of them are in their thirties and pretty fast. I have tried to react to their moves when I am one-on-one with them, but commonly, they blow past me, and I find myself already one to two steps behind before I'm able to react and start chasing them. There are other guys with whom I can keep up, but after getting back into competitive soccer nine months ago, I find myself almost resigned to the thought that perhaps I am not going to be like I was in my thirties or forties. I would say I peaked playing soccer in my late twenties, and that era, for sure, is long gone.

At times, I feel that I need a good dose of daydreaming. My memory brings me back to those days of running without end and playing as if the day would last forever, a reenactment that seems to take place now and makes me feel young again. But then I think about all the battles that my body has endured, and I feel old again. Like a B-17 bomber in World War II, I have many holes in the fuselage from soccer-injured broken bones, tuberculosis as a child, cancer and its two relapses, spinal stenosis with a herniated disc that gives me tingling and numbness sensations in my left foot, having my gallbladder removed, dealing with a monoclonal antibody that could be the precursor to multiple myeloma, arthritis in the right ankle and right big toe from soccer, and now, lately, the left-knee issue. I realize that I have aged.

These thoughts and memories bring me close to God while I keep an eye on the traffic. My vision in prayer takes me back to Cali, Colombia, and going up to Cristo Rey with my friends, as I did so many times when I was in my young teen years. Cristo Rey is a white statue of Jesus, about eighty-seven feet tall, made of iron and concrete. It sits on a mountain at an altitude of about 4,600 feet, just west of the city, which is at an elevation of about 3,300 feet in the Cauca Valley in between the Andes Mountain ranges. This statue of Jesus is similar to the statue of Jesus in Rio de Janeiro but smaller in size. For no other reason than to feel the need to exercise and want to conquer a difficult challenge, we would sometimes run up the mountain to see the statue of Jesus up close and drink a bottle of Coca-Cola when we got there. We would run from home on city streets, cross a main road, and then go to the road up the mountain. But instead of taking the side-winding road, we would shoot straight up. The landscape would change from city streets lined by houses made of brick and mortar with clay shingles, to dirt roads lined by houses made of wood with metal roofs, to dirt paths lined by grass and bushes, until we got to the top. It would take us about sixty minutes to climb up but about fifteen to twenty minutes to run down.

As I ran up on the dirt trails in between brush and trees and passing by chickens and dogs, I began to see Jesus, higher up in front of me, with Peter, James, and John. I slowed down to a walking pace and kept my distance from them. Jesus had been entrenched in his mission work and had just appointed the twelve disciples to follow him. According to the Gospel of Luke, he also had performed the miracle of feeding five thousand, beginning with five loaves and two fish.

I reached the top of the mountain and immediately looked up at the statue of Jesus. It looked so tall as I stood by its feet. I then turned around, walked toward the guard rail, and looked down at the city. In the foreground, I could see the dirt trail we had just come up and the green grass with trees and bushes in between. In the background, the city was dotted with red clay-shingle roofs, tall buildings of red brick and some with white plaster, and buses and taxis on the roads. Interestingly enough, I could not hear a single beep from them. It was quiet up there, and I could feel a gentle breeze on my arms. The city in the 1970s had a population of about 800,000 people, so it looked pretty large from where I stood. With the statue of Jesus behind me as I looked at the city, I was in awe of how big everything seemed in comparison to my size.

I then looked at Jesus as he knelt and prayed, and he began to transfigure himself. As Luke recounts in 9:28–36, "As he was praying, the appearance of his face changed, and his clothes became as bright as a flash of lightning" (Luke 9:29). There was purity in his being, and God glorified him while in the presence of Moses and Elijah. I felt a sense of peace and love. For that moment, I was one with Jesus and became oblivious to the world, although, oddly enough, I still kept my car in its lane. There was nothing that I needed. I just wanted to rest with Jesus and the Father in communion with the Holy Spirit. I was tempted, like Peter, to ask if I should build a tent so we could remain there. Instead, I just rested in Jesus's presence. He then looked at me, and I could feel his presence in me. His brown eyes placed me in such awe that it became hard to take a deep breath. I could feel him calling me and saying, "I love you, John, and you are mine." I felt a deep ache in my throat, and my eyes began to water as he made me feel special. I remained thoughtless for the moment.

Seeing Jesus's transfiguration in my prayer brought me back to the times when I would lie by the pool I frequented as a teen. Cali had held the Pan-American games in 1971, and the city had built a fifty-meter, Olympic-size pool. Mom would give me money to spend an afternoon there every so often, and I would escape to the pool to swim and lie beside it, basking in the sun. During those times, I could feel my body get warm, and I could visualize my body become dazzlingly bright, beginning in the center of my chest and belly and outward to my arms and legs. My face would be the last part to radiate with rays of sun. I felt pure, as if God was healing me from the stresses of life.

Still deep in prayer, I could see myself running down the mountain. I looked at my body one more time and realized that it was still strong. Despite the damage and holes in the fuselage, this shell still housed my soul. While feeling the love and presence of Jesus in me, I began to appreciate that this body was actually a holy temple for God. I had learned this in school when I was younger, but today, I could actually feel that concept in my heart.

My thoughts transitioned with Saint Paul's writing to the Corinthians in his first letter:

> Don't you know that you yourselves are God's temple and that God's Spirit dwells in your midst? If anyone destroys God's temple, God will destroy that person; for God's temple is sacred, and you together are that temple. (1 Corinthians, 3:16–17)

Putting context into this writing, Saint Paul is addressing the people of Corinth as a whole and referring to them as the church, the holy temple of God. But these words have influenced me at a personal level as well, and I too see my body as a temple where God's Holy Spirit dwells.

I have come to appreciate our bodies, whether male or female, as vessels for our souls and without need to see them in a sexual manner. Our world and culture put a lot of pressure on us to see ourselves in an inappropriately and distorted sexual manner, and sometimes we mistreat ourselves because of this pressure. I succumbed to these temptations many times in my youth. During my high school and college years, I looked at *Playboy* and *Penthouse* magazines with my friends. On a couple of occasions, I went to X-rated movies. It seemed as if this was a rite of passage for us boys before we matured. I'm not sure why this happened to us, but I do believe that this process of male development has led to a disrespect of women.

The #MeToo movement has been building momentum for quite some time and appropriately so; it is in full force at this time. We fathers have to do a better job with our sons in teaching them to respect girls and women. If this confession has made you feel uncomfortable and disrespected, please accept my apologies from the bottom of my heart. I have learned and changed from those younger days and have made it a point, when I'm in the office, to talk about values with the preteens and adolescents.

My prayer came to an end as I exited the highway. I felt that God had given me a gift—to really appreciate our bodies as they were meant to be. Whether these vessels were riddled with brokenness from age, disease, arthritis, or impure thoughts and actions, God wanted me to take care of my body with respect and with healthy choices for sleep, food, and exercise, as it was a holy temple of God.

But this realization remained idle for a time as we moved from the warm summer months to the fall season. I came to appreciate that God wanted me to see my body as a holy temple for God's presence, no matter how my body felt as it aged. I felt that God was taking care of it and would transfigure it in the future, when the time was right. I was left with a feeling that there was more that God wanted to say to me, but I didn't know what it was. I had to let time pass and trust that God would talk to me again with perhaps other experiences.

The fall season came into full bloom, and then the leaves fell off the trees. My left knee healed, and the swelling and stiffness resolved. I had felt a little empty in my understanding of my body as a temple for God after writing the beginning of this chapter in July. Concurrently, as I write again in November, I have not been able to play soccer for the past three weeks. My left ankle, which used to be the "good one," has been hurting to the point that I sometimes limp when I walk. An x-ray earlier this week revealed some arthritis and bone spurs. I recalled trying to play a few days ago but only lasted ten minutes because of the pain. As I leaned my back and head against one of the walls at the soccer complex and closed my eyes, all I could think about was the time and effort I had put in to making a comeback from my left-knee injury and feeling some frustration. My game had improved over the summer to the point that I had started dribbling again, and I was scoring goals. But that night at the soccer complex, reality was sinking in that I was going to have to take some time off to allow my ankle to heal. That meant getting out of shape, at least from the soccer point of view. My ball skill was going to become stiff and awkward again. I could tell that some anxiety wanted to pop up. I even wondered if I was going to have to give up soccer for good. Frustration sank in that night, but it was tempered as I found myself in conversation with God, feeling better that God understood my point of view.

I took the dogs out to go potty the following morning, fed them, and then went outside again to pick up after them. As I walked down the driveway and to the sidewalk, I contemplated the gray sky and barren trees, and I breathed the fresh, crisp air. My left ankle ached a little, but I felt God's presence with love and peace in this walk.

Being in God's presence, I then found myself with Peter and the other disciples by the beach as Jesus was cooking some fish.

It was after the Resurrection, and the disciples had just realized they were with the resurrected Jesus.

> When they had finished eating, Jesus said to Simon Peter, "Simon son of John, do you love me more than these?" "Yes, Lord," he said, "you know that I love you." Jesus said, "Feed my lambs." (John 21:15)

Jesus proceeded to ask Peter two more times if Peter loved him, and it was at this moment that I realized what God had been trying to tell me since July. I had come to appreciate my body as a holy temple of God in the summer, despite everything that I had been through in my life. But God was asking me to go deeper in my understanding of my body as it related to God. Even if I had just discovered one more ailment in my body with the left-ankle arthritis and the subsequent emotions that went with it, God was asking me, "John, do you love me more than these anxieties; these worries and frustrations that you have about your body; this pain that you have?"

I let the question sink in for a bit. I then replied, "Yes, Lord, you know that I love you."

"John, do you love me more than your body?"

And I replied once more, "Yes, Lord, you know that I love you."

Yet a third time: "John, do you love me more than yourself?" This question was deeper yet, and it required that I contemplate myself a little more slowly. It then became natural to feel that I could renounce myself. It didn't matter what I had been through or what I was dealing with at the present. I felt that God was asking me to see my broken body as a temple for God but to then step out of it and renounce it so that my soul could unite itself with God. All I could feel then was that I belonged to God, and I just wanted to rest in God's arms. With a smile in my heart and not wanting to be distressed like Peter was, I said, "Yes, Lord, I will always love you."

At this point, my eyes got watery. I felt engulfed in God's arms and felt the love, despite how my body felt—old, with surgical scars, and arthritic. And then God said to me, "I call you by name, and you are mine." I simply rested without any thoughts as I walked back to the house.

Sometimes we feel like the story of Israel in the Old Testament, don't we? Sometimes Israel would find itself in trouble with God, and God would come in and save them, showering them with love, while trying to bring them closer. I think we all have had times of pain, be it physical, emotional, or spiritual, that have caused us distress. If we are sensitive enough, we could feel God come in afterward and display affection toward us. God so wants to take care of us, to hold us, and to let us know that we are loved. Nothing would make God happier than if we recognized this and let God into our hearts.

On this journey, I have experienced physical pain but mostly, I have grieved my aging body. I think underneath all this at subconscious level, I have been longing to have back my youth and my ability to do sports: I peaked and played my best soccer in my late twenties, when I was playing in Chicago in an open league. I ran my best in my early twenties when running a 7:30 minute/mile average in a 10K run and an eight minute/mile on a ten-mile run. But God has helped me see the transition of my aging body, while my love for God has gone deeper in my heart. Today, God the Father and God the Son have illuminated me with their Holy Spirit and love. Gratitude then sinks in.

Thank you, Lord, for taking care of me. You have helped me take care of my body, and despite my brokenness, you are always with me, trying to make me whole. You have been with me in all my ailments, all my surgeries, and all my pain. You give me your love and peace, and the least I can do is offer my body back to you as a sacrifice of enduring pain and emotions because I love you more than these.

# Part 3

Part 3

# Chapter 21

# You Are My Rock

*January 2019*

We had some cold weather and snow toward the end of November and beginning of December, but the snow melted before Christmas, as the temperature went back into the forties. The multicolored Christmas lights on the trees and the Santa, angels, Snoopy, and Jesus decorations on the houses brought a sense of joy and anticipation as we waited for the birth of Jesus on the twenty-fifth. But it was also that time of the year to have my blood drawn.

There is nothing more humbling for me than to get my blood drawn every six months to make sure that my testicular cancer is not coming back and that this monoclonal antibody I have is not going to increase any further to give me the diagnosis of multiple myeloma.

Even though I know the routine and I prepare myself, mentally and emotionally, on those mornings, and I have been doing so every six months for the past thirty-two years, I feel that I lose my joy in my heart during the time it takes me to drive to the hospital, get my blood drawn, and then wait for the results later that day. I always get anxious and feel a little nervous, although I try to remain in control. It feels as if I lose my identity, and it does not matter who I am because there is that potential that I may die from cancer; then I will no longer be. I cease to be the soccer player who scored so many goals. I am no longer the pediatrician who helped children get better. I stop being the husband to my wife and the father to my children. I enter an area where I don't have any friends to whom I can talk. In a way, I become stripped of my clothing and stand completely naked with nothing to protect me, and that's when I become most vulnerable in my life. It would be easy to think that I might fall into despair and sadness.

Yet it is during these times when God rescues me, and I feel closest to God. On those days when I have my blood drawn, I pray silently with God, feeling God's touch and appreciating, one more time, that God engulfs me in God's arms. It is during these times when I feel so vulnerable that I acknowledge, in the deepest part of my heart, that I am totally dependent on God. If I happen to be at work, examining children, I can most easily see how God works through me to take care of them, and it is not my doing at all. If I'm home, it is God's love that is passed on to my wife and children, and it's not my doing at all. If I'm playing in a soccer game, I experience the freedom of the Holy Spirit as I dribble the ball, take shots, and run here and there, and I realize that it is not me at all. During those days, I stand face-to-face with God and let God decide if I should continue to live or not. I have no guarantees to live longer, and oddly enough, I find myself in such a peaceful state that I actually feel I can give up my life, then and now, and just be with God. It would be OK for me to die, and I know that Anne, Tim, and Patty would be OK. On those days, I hear God say to me, "John, you are my beloved son with whom I am well pleased," and I simply rest.

It is at this point, after I have been absorbed into the business of the world, that I realize that I have forgotten my true identity. While it is true that I play soccer, I take care of children in the office, and I am a father and husband, God tugs at me one more time, asking,

"John, who are you?" I then realize, one more time in the depths of my heart, my true identity: I am God's beloved son, and God calls me by name. I belong to God, and God belongs to me, deep in my heart.

As the day went along at work, and I saw children for routine care and for ill visits, I waited for the results, which eventually came at the end of the day: the tumor markers were in the normal range. There was relief and reassurance once more that I was simply here to be God's messenger and helper. Life is not about me but about my brothers and sisters. The gifts of healing that I have as a pediatrician don't belong to me but to the babies, children, adolescents, and young adults for whom I care. I pass on these gifts of healing to them, letting God work through me. And nothing gives me more joy than to feel that I have learned to get out of the way to let God do God's job.

A week later, however, the results of the monoclonal antibody came back, and the results were a little higher than six months ago. Fear came back, and I felt unsettled. On that day when I was at work, I began to have many thoughts and feelings of insecurity. I don't know why, after feeling like I was at peace the previous week and could give myself totally to God, I then felt like I was not ready to die. I couldn't tell if it was related to thinking my children still needed me. Maybe Anne needed me. I wondered if I was feeling their sadness and that was holding me back. I wondered if children at the office still needed me to take care of them. Did I still belong here?

That evening, as I found time to type on my iPad in between seeing patients, I found myself all over the place with my thoughts and emotions. I listened to very different genres of music from the iPad, from smooth jazz to spa music to Jimmy Buffett, but I could not find any satisfaction. I wanted to run away from myself, but I couldn't. I felt trapped. After seeing patients that evening, I shared my results with a coworker and shed some tears. And later that night, I came home and talked with Anne and shed some more tears.

Later that week, I found myself in prayer in Caesarea Philippi, with Jesus and the disciples. Caesarea Philippi was a city about twenty miles north of the Sea of Galilee. According to the Gospel of Matthew, Jesus had already performed the miracles of feeding five thousand and four thousand. As he was in the middle of his ministry, he had performed multiple healings. He was about to talk to them about his passion and wanted to ascertain what they knew of him:

> When Jesus came to the region of Caesarea Philippi, he asked his disciples, "Who do people say the Son of Man is?"
>
> They replied, "Some say John the Baptist; others say Elijah; and still others, Jeremiah or one of the prophets."
>
> "But what about you?" he asked. "Who do you say I am?"
>
> Simon Peter answered, "You are the Messiah, the Son of the living God."
>
> Jesus replied, "Blessed are you, Simon son of Jonah, for this was not revealed to you by flesh and blood, but by my Father in heaven. And I tell you that you are Peter, and on this rock I will build my church, and the gates of Hades will not overcome it." (Matthew 16:13–18)

As I contemplated this passage and saw Jesus assigning Peter as the rock upon whom he was going to build his church, I saw Anne in my life as a rock of steadiness and stability. Anne and I have different temperaments and do things differently, from how we do the dishes, to how we hang clothes from the dryer, to how we hang toilet paper in the bathroom, to name a few. But we love each other unconditionally, and she has found ways to help me become the person that God made me out to be, just as I do for her. We share many likes, from our mutual interests in travel and, in particular, appreciating the French culture and going to southern France, to playing sports, to reading and having many intellectual discussions, among others. I love her inclination for art, from writing to drawing and painting. She helps bring out in me that part that is artistic as well. I can play the guitar and sing, but I do so horribly. However, singing and playing the guitar make my heart happy.

It is her steadiness and desire to achieve in sports, just as I do, that helps her plow through life's difficult problems and come out on the other end. And so, in moments of uncertainty with my cancer, I have found Anne to be my rock, as God illuminates her and inspires her through the Holy Spirit. God helps me in prayer, and Anne sustains me in the day-to-day challenges, as far back as when we were dating and I had my first bout with testicular cancer in 1985, to the relapses in 1998 and 2000, to now dealing with this monoclonal protein and wondering if I will develop multiple myeloma. Her help has been as challenging for her as helping me recover post-operatively by helping me walk, go to the bathroom, bathe me, feed me, and tell me silly jokes in moments of despair and feeling beaten down. It has been in this state of humility, where I have allowed Anne to help me, that I have realized that God has been working through her to take care of me. Love flowing from God to Anne but also flowing from God to me through Anne.

Thank you, God, for giving me the opportunity to meet Anne at the end of my sophomore year of college, answering my prayer in church that I was ready to meet the girl with whom I wanted to spend the rest of my life. Thank you for illuminating us and guiding us in difficult times and for giving us hope that you will be with us, no matter the circumstances of life.

# Chapter 22

# Yearning for My Identity

*February 2019*

Now that I find time in February to do more typing, I find myself more settled. This monoclonal protein is turning out to be my next challenge in life and in my relationship with God. I have had an opportunity to pray better with God and find some peace in my heart. It is during the times of confusion and pain that I find God most helpful, to guide me, to console me, to hold me in God's arms, and to let me know it's going to be OK. It is during these times that I'm reminded that I might not like having a drink from this cup, but it is God's will that must be done, and I'm able to acquiesce to God's will because I feel love from God, and I love God back.

I have come to appreciate that this relationship with God is essential to my life, not only to feel God as my sustenance to life but also in helping me find out who I am, as God made me to be. In the depths of my heart, I yearn to know myself, to find out who I am and how I fit in in this world. It is only in my relatedness to God that I can find out who I truly am, my true self.

As I meditated and prayed about this, I found myself in Capernaum with the crowd as we followed Jesus. According to the Gospel of Matthew, Jesus had already undergone the three temptations by the devil (chapter 4) and had started his ministry (chapter 5). He gave the Sermon on the Mount (chapter 5) and talked about prayer and Christian practices (chapters 6 and 7). People were healed and demons were cast out. As Saint Mark states in his gospel: "News about him spread quickly over the whole region of Galilee" (Mark 1:28).

Caught up in the heat of midday, I had sweat on my forehead, and my clothing felt sticky. The air felt dry, and the sun was bearing down. I was a little hungry because I had skipped lunch. People were buying food at the small market tables, and other financial deals were being made. Diagonally from me, I could see Matthew (also called Levi in the Gospels of Luke and Mark), working busily as he collected taxes from people. Jesus approached his table. "'Follow me,' he told him, and Matthew got up and followed him" (Matthew 9:9).

The Gospels of Mark and Luke recount the same encounter, and they use almost the same words. The Gospel of Mark says "As he walked along, he saw Levi son of Alphaeus sitting at the tax collector's booth. 'Follow me,' Jesus told him, and Levi got up and followed him" (Mark 2:14).

The Gospel of Luke says, "After this, Jesus went out and saw a tax collector by the name of Levi sitting at his tax booth. 'Follow me,' Jesus said to him, and Levi got up, left everything and followed him" (Luke 5:27–28).

If I hadn't found myself in prayer almost two millennia ago, I would have thought that Jesus had used his Jedi powers on Matthew. I could almost see Jesus extending his arm as he pointed at Matthew and saying, "Follow me," and Matthew saying in reply, "Yes, Master, I will follow you."

What kind of a spell did Jesus use on Matthew, where there was little exchange of words and it was all action? As I thought about this, I thought about how powerful God's grace is that he can change our hearts on a dime. If we put this picture in context, Jesus had already started choosing his disciples but had not approached Matthew yet, as Jesus probably knew that Matthew was not ready. Being a tax collector in those days, Matthew probably had some greed and probably some other not-so-nice things in his heart. In addition, as Mark says in his gospel, "News about him spread quickly over the whole region of Galilee." Matthew, coming in contact with many people because of his position, had to know of Jesus's fame. But Matthew was not ready to follow Jesus until that personal encounter with Jesus. And as they locked eyes on each other, Matthew's heart melted as he became engulfed in Jesus's mercy, forgiveness, and love—God's grace in action! Thus, with Jesus's company, Matthew began to see himself in a different light, as an apostle being charged with distributing God's love all over and leaving behind his tax-collection duties. This was his new identity in the presence of God.

Sometimes God gets our attention suddenly, or, as Saint Mark likes to use in his gospel, "immediately." I also think about Saint Paul, when he converted after having his personal encounter with Jesus. For me, I felt like the call was gradual, as I started to feel close to God after my first Communion and then at the age of twelve after confirmation, when I started going to church by myself. My following intensified, however, when I started having my cancer relapses. And as I got closer to God, I discovered myself better as a son of God, my true identity.

Using God as a backdrop, I have been taking an assessment of myself, with all my positive qualities and negative attributes. Because it may seem abstract that I cannot see God with my own eyes, I have learned to see in Jesus what I could possibly be like. Developing this relationship with Jesus has been helpful to me. At the Last Supper (John 13–14), Jesus is talking to the disciples and asking them to maintain their faith in God and Jesus and to love one another. He then says to them that he is going to leave them, and then,

Simon Peter asked him, "Lord, where are you going?"
Jesus replied, "Where I am going, you cannot follow
now, but you will follow later." (John 13:36)

Later,

Thomas said to him, "Lord, we don't know where
you are going, so how can we know the way?" Jesus
answered, "I am the way and the truth and the life.
No one comes to the Father except through me."
(John 14:5–6)

So I follow Jesus and learn from him, as he is God and the way
to God. And in knowing how Jesus acted and what he taught us, I
can see myself truthfully as I am and accept myself as I am.

I have come to appreciate that I have to be honest with myself if
I want to discover myself. This is especially so if I don't get positive
feedback from people, and this stirs in my heart emotions that
seem to be negative. I may want to repress those feelings or simply
run away from myself as I make myself busy in other activities.
Sometimes I get distracted or confused about how people perceive
me. What I have noticed through the years is that the more grounded
I am with God, the better I know myself in a truthful manner, and
the less likely I am to be distracted as I see myself as perceived by
others. I can see myself better as I relate to God, the only source of
the truth. Then, my heart feels at peace, even when things don't
seem to be going well, as has happened recently with the latest
results of this monoclonal antibody. Stressful events like this tend
to destabilize me.

People around me help me discover myself. Not only do I learn
about myself when I get feedback from them, but they want to see
me improve. In God's divine providence, I get feedback from people
around me as to how I am doing with my actions and thoughts. If I
use God's love and mercy as a backdrop, I can ascertain the validity

151

of people's feedback and then institute change to help me become a better person. In addition, my family and friends praying for me helps me change. Their spiritual power influences my spiritual world and helps me line up better with God. And my guardian angels and the saints also intercede on my behalf to help me change. It is in this state of love and mercy, being in communion with the saints and with my friends and family, that I can become the person who God made me to be. When I fulfill this promise, joy permeates my heart and God's heart, and then I feel God telling me one more time, "Come, John, follow me," and without hesitation, I stand up and follow Jesus in my new identity.

I feel very lucky that God pointed me in the direction to become a pediatrician, to discover my vocation. It gives me joy to take care of children, to help them get better from illnesses, and to help them develop appropriately. But recognizing in my heart that my true identity is being a child of God makes me feel fulfilled. It is in this spot that I find love and peace.

Thank you, Jesus, for helping me with my identity to help me realize that I am a son of God. This satisfies my yearning in the depths of my heart to discover myself. It is in this state that I can pass on your love and mercy better.

# Chapter 23

# Yearning for Love and God

*February 2019*

> The Force is what gives a Jedi his power. It's an
> energy field created by all living things. It surrounds
> us and penetrates us. It binds the Galaxy together.
> —Jedi Master Obi-Wan Kenobi
> *Star Wars Episode IV: A New Hope*

It was the summer of 1978 when I graduated from high school in Colombia and decided to come back to the United States. I had mentioned to Dad that I was interested in continuing my college education in the States and was possibly contemplating doing medicine as a career. George Lucas decided to release his *Star Wars* series in 1977, starting with *Episode IV*, introducing to the public these concepts of a Jedi Master, the Force, and good versus evil. I had heard about the *Star Wars* movie and that it was made with different and unusual characters, with a sci-fi theme to it. After Dad and I decided it would be a good idea for me to repeat another year of high school to help me relearn English, he took my brother and me to the theater later in the fall to see the movie. I missed that famous quote the first time I watched it, but it has made an impression on me after having watched the movie multiple times.

After thinking about my monoclonal antibody in December and meditating and praying in January, I came to appreciate, one more time, the influence that God has had on my life. This spiritual force surrounds me and penetrates me. I see God everywhere I look, albeit sometimes I get caught up in the fast pace of life and have difficulty seeing the other person with love and mercy. As I thought about this, I found myself, one more time, in meditation and prayer.

Jesus had arrived in Capernaum, a fishing village in the northern part of the Sea of Galilee. He was in the middle of his ministry, giving advice on prayer and behavior and curing the sick, and he was getting closer to his passion. He had already shown himself in the transfiguration to Peter, James, and John (Matthew 17). Sitting by the sea, listening to the waves and feeling the cool breeze passing through my shirt, I attentively listened to Jesus. Children ran by on the sand and dirt, and Jesus had just placed one of them on his lap, saying, "Truly I tell you, unless you change and become like little children, you will never enter the kingdom of heaven. Therefore, whoever takes the lowly position of this child is the greatest in the kingdom of heaven" (Matthew 18:3–4).

He was teaching his disciples about temptation and sin (Matthew 18) and wanted to emphasize the mercy that God has for us when we fall. He talked about the parable of the servant who had to settle his accounts with the king, after Peter had asked him if seven times was enough to forgive someone. Jesus replied, "I tell you, not seven times, but seventy-seven times" (Matthew 18:22).

I have found that love and mercy go hand in hand. As part of learning who I am and what I can bring to the table, I often find faults and weaknesses in myself as I use God as a backdrop, in full honesty of myself and in the truth, which is God. But in prayer, usually when I'm in contemplative prayer, I feel God's mercy and

God being understanding of my errors and forgiving me, not just seven times but seventy times seven.

There have been times when I have not been merciful and understanding in my heart. I have had, in psychological terms, *reaction formations*. These reactions happened when situations or actions came up and stirred emotions in my heart that caused distress or anxiety, and I perceived these feelings to be unacceptable. I thus reacted in the opposite direction, giving me what would be called a reaction formation. For example, if somebody at work created in my heart feelings of distrust and contempt, my subsequent thought or feeling would be that this was not a nice reaction or feeling. I therefore reacted outwardly in a positive and trustful way so as to conceal my original feelings. I appeared nice on the outside, but I was not nice in the inside with those feelings of distrust and contempt. More deeply, I probably failed to see the other person in God's image, good and wonderful as he or she is, yet human like me, capable of making mistakes. I fell short of being understanding and merciful.

As I looked out toward the sea and contemplated the horizon, with the sun setting, I thought about God bathing me in God's love and helping me dissipate this love in an effortless manner, full of freedom and without physical or emotional attachments, as I let the Holy Spirit guide me. I do so in the face of mercy, as God has been merciful with me too. I have to ask God to accept me as I am, in my full humanity, so that I can feel peace and love one more time. And so I am learning how to accept the people around me, as they are in their full humanity. They make mistakes, just like I make mistakes, and I can be merciful and understanding, just like God has been merciful and understanding of me. It is in this state of humility and mercy that I can be bound to people, being side by side, sharing our trust and love for each other, as we try to make our world a better place to live.

As I continued to sit on the rock, listening to Jesus, feeling the breeze and watching the children run and play, I thought about all the children that I have taken care of. At times, I feel lucky that God pointed me in the direction to be a pediatrician because it has been in taking care of children that I have found joy. This was all God's plan, and I just fit in. But seeing Jesus with his disciples and engaging in play with the children, I feel my identity is also as a child of God, as I too try to pass on love, mercy, and joy to others.

I feel that in the depths of my heart, I have two main yearnings: I yearn to find my identity, and I yearn for love. When I realize both of these yearnings in relationship with God, then my heart feels at peace.

This relationship with Jesus and God helps me realize myself as God made me out to be. When I don't do well in this relationship, or I don't engage in it at all, I am likely to express my actions from my yearnings in a distorted manner and feel unfulfilled in the depths of my heart. I have a difficult time finding out who I am, and I search for love in unfulfilling ways. I let the material world satisfy me and try to make me happy, or I search for happiness in other people, who, being imperfect themselves, give me love in an imperfect way. This distortion in my yearnings not only adversely affects me in my behavior, but it also adversely affects my relationships with others.

When I do well in this relationship with God, I feel God's love and peace in the depths of my heart. I feel fulfilled to the point that I feel I am at home, my true home. In prayer, I cast aside all worries and anxieties. I let my guard down, acknowledging that God is all powerful, and God can take care of me. I place myself at God's disposal and simply ask God to guide me in being a servant because I often don't know the right thing to do. Then, the wind comes under my wings and lets me take flight, going anywhere, as the Holy Spirit can go here or there, and it is always right.

Feeling God's love, I can't help but pass this love on to everybody else. I then find myself in better communion with the saints and practice better mercy and acts of charity. I want to be as holy as God is holy and as perfect as God is perfect. I have an even deeper craving for the transfiguration and the desire to go home. This wonderful state of love, all of God's doing, is for God alone. When I go to church or I pray at home, it is all for God, and anything that I may do that has a positive outcome is not of my own doing; it is not me at all.

This relationship, this yearning for love and satisfaction in the heart, happens in prayer. It is in this communication that I feel one with God. Prayer has changed for me as I have developed spiritually and as I have deepened my relationship with God. I have gone from mental prayer (reciting prayers) to meditative prayer (prayer in my intellect) to contemplative prayer (speechless prayer in my heart), although I will disclaim that I am still learning how to pray. There are times when I don't go into contemplative prayer but might remain in mental prayer or meditative prayer, depending on how busy I feel.

Perhaps what I have learned, most importantly, over the past two decades is to pray to honor God and to persevere in prayer, even when things don't seem to be going well, or I seem to not have enough time. I may pray to God to ask for something in particular, but more important, in the midst of these difficult times, I don't let anxiety get the best of me; I love God, honor God, and am reverent toward God. And just as important, I have learned to not get complacent in prayer when life is going smoothly, and things seem to be going well. If anything, I have become more thankful in my prayer under these positive circumstances, experiencing gratitude toward God.

As I look at Jesus one last time, I say thank you, Jesus, for leading me to Capernaum and letting me listen to you. You help me in my self-discovery, and you help me feel your love. In experiencing this love freely, I am able to pass on this love freely to others. This love permeates our world, and if I can set aside my pride and have mercy for others, I can let this love penetrate us and bind our world. In having love and mercy in my heart, I can work with those who surround me with respect and dignity. I can help them become the persons that God meant for them to be.

Thank you, God, for placing me in this world so that I can make our world a better place to live. Thank you for helping me realize that change in our world will only happen if I can make change happen in my heart, as I develop a relationship with you and your Son, Jesus, and as I let the Holy Spirit guide me wherever it wants to take me.

# Chapter 24

# Epilogue

*January 2020*

I t is my hope that this book will be helpful to you as you contemplate your relationship with God. I initially began to write it for Tim and Patty, as I thought I was going to die while I was having my testicular cancer relapses in between 1998 and 2000. As it turns out, I am still alive, and so I have kept on writing. The monoclonal antibody that we have been following has gradually increased over the past seven years, but clinically, I still don't have the diagnosis of multiple myeloma and thus retain the diagnosis of MGUS (monoclonal gammopathy of unknown significance). Perhaps you have had an experience in life that has put you at the crossroads of what is important in life, and that's why you picked up this book. My interpretation of this would be that God is gently nudging you, gently calling you to "come and see" what this relationship is all about.

Fr. James Martin, in his book *Jesus: A Pilgrimage*,[22] talks about this relationship. In John 1:26–39, John the Baptist is explaining to some Pharisees about the one who is greater than him, and then:

The next day John saw Jesus coming toward him and said, "Look, the Lamb of God, who takes away the sin of the world! This is the one I meant when I said, 'A man who comes after me has surpassed me because he was before me.' I myself did not know him, but the reason I came baptizing with water was that he might be revealed to Israel." (John 1:29–31)

Two disciples who are with John the Baptist want to develop a new relationship with Jesus after they hear John the Baptist say that Jesus is the Lamb of God.

When the two disciples heard him say this, they followed Jesus. Turning around, Jesus saw them following and asked, "What do you want?"

They said, "Rabbi" (which means "Teacher"), "where are you staying?"

"Come," he replied, "and you will see."

So, they went and saw where he was staying, and they spent that day with him. It was about four in the afternoon." (John 1:37–39)

As Fr. James Martin explains, Jesus did not give them a long dissertation about life with God but rather said, "Come and you will see."

Similarly, Pope Benedict XVI comments on the same event in his book, *Benedictus: Day by Day with Pope Benedict XVI*:

For the disciples, it was the beginning of a direct acquaintance with the Teacher, seeing where he was staying and starting to get to know him. Indeed, they were not to proclaim an idea, but to witness to a person. Before being sent out to preach, they had to "be" with Jesus, establishing a personal relationship with him. [23]

Jesus is asking us to have a personal relationship with him where sometimes words fall short of communication, and we simply talk in the heart with "groanings of love," as Saint Paul said in his letter to the Romans.

My journey toward God not only has been aided by having a relationship with Jesus but also by having a relationship with the saints and family members who have passed away and are interceding on my behalf (I'm thinking of my grandma Murphy) and by those who are here with me, as God has worked through them for my benefit, and they have prayed for me. Here, in this life, it has been my friends from medical school at my bedside, praying for me when I was going through chemotherapy and surgeries; the surgeons, nurses, and oncologists who took care of me as I battled my cancer and its relapses; the oncology nurse who gave nutrition information to Anne to help me while I was getting chemotherapy; the Regos family in Chicago who prayed for me; Anne's parents, her brothers and sister, and her friend Sharon, who not only prayed but also helped out with day-to-day activities; the parents at my son's St. Augustine Elementary School, who prayed in church for me while I was going through my relapses; Pauline, a Christian Scientist and a very devout person, who guided me initially in the direction of daily prayer; and Anne, Tim, and Patty, who gave me their unconditional love, took care of the day-to-day activities, and helped me heal during my relapses. All of them, through God's grace, intervened to help me stay alive but have become the woven fabric to help me in the development of my relationship with God. It is because of them, as part of my relationship with God, that I am who I am today.

Along the way, I hope you may let your guard down and allow God to touch your heart, to give you a big embrace, and to let you know that you are his beloved son or daughter, with whom he is well pleased. And just as God accepts you as you are and where you are,

I hope that you will begin to accept yourself as you are and where you are. Despite whatever deficiencies you feel you have, God still hugs you and says to you, "You are my beloved son or daughter, with whom I am well pleased."

At the end of the day, it all comes down to love. When it is time for me to die, I will be unclothed and vulnerable, without any material possessions; I will only have what is in my memory, intellect, and heart. And what remains in my heart is the presence of God, my feeling of God's love for me, and the love I have for God. It's a love that is accompanied by humility and meekness and is full of reverence as I acknowledge that God is my creator, to whom I long to return. So I work on this concept while I am still on earth, and hopefully, I will not be too far behind in my spiritual development at the time of my death.

I am simply a vessel that allows God's love to flow through, and I pass this love to my wife and kids. Through this love, I hope I can carry out works of charity, mercy, and healing to the kids and parents I take care of in the office. And I pass this love to those I do not know but I see on the streets, those who are in need, because they are also my brothers and sisters. They are God's children too.

There have been times when I wished I had an aptitude for poetry. I admire those who can use words so beautifully to describe what is in their souls. I have read the works of Saint John of the Cross several times, gradually understanding them better each time I read them, but I still feel the need to reread them every so often. Saint John of the Cross (1542–1591) was a Spanish poet and mystic, a Carmelite priest who wrote of his relationship with God in poetry. Four works stand out from his writings: "The Ascent of Mount Carmel," "The Dark Night," "The Spiritual Canticle," and "The Living Flame of Love."

I have needed to read others' works to understand better Saint John of the Cross. I read Iain Matthew's *The Impact of God: Soundings from St. John of the Cross*,[24] which helped me understand better the last work of Saint John of the Cross, "The Living Flame of Love" I also read Kieran Kavanaugh's book, *John of the Cross: Doctor of Light and Love*.[25]

As Saint John of the Cross has been with me in so many instances, both in some of my darkest nights and during those times when my heart was flaming with God's love, I would like to close this book with a tribute to him by quoting his poem "The Living Flame of Love." As Kieran Kavanaugh says in his book, it is "a song of the soul in the intimate communication of loving union with God"[25]:

O living flame of love
That tenderly wounds my soul
In its deepest center! Since
Now you are not oppressive,
Now consummate! If it be your will:
Tear through the veil of this sweet encounter!

O sweet cautery,
O delightful wound,
O gentle hand! O delicate touch
That tastes of eternal life
And pays every debt!
In killing you changed death to life.

O lamps of fire!
In whose splendors
The deep caverns of feeling,
Once obscure and blind,
Now give forth, so rarely, so exquisitely,
Both warmth and light to their Beloved.

How gently and lovingly
You wake in my heart,
Where in secret you dwell alone;
And in your sweet breathing,
Filled with good and glory,
How tenderly you swell my heart with love.

# Acknowledgments

I would like to thank the following groups of people:

To my wife, Anne, for being my buddy and my companion on this journey that we have traveled together, and for being so supportive—you have been my rock and steady hand. Your input and editing knowledge have helped shape this book, especially in those parts where it seemed that my Spanish and English syntax were getting mixed up. But most importantly, through the years, you have helped me to see that God's love engulfs us both as we navigate through life together, and to see that my relationship with God is as important as my relationship with you.

You also helped me acknowledge that my relationship with God included all those times when friends, classmates, and relatives were involved in my care. When I first wrote this book, I was focused in my prayer and relationship with God, to the extent that the book was initially about those topics only, and I did not acknowledge those around me. Although I understood this concept in God's divine providence, you helped me see that my relationship with God in his divine providence, with our friends, classmates, and relatives, needed to be included in the book, as they had become part of the woven fabric of my relationship with God.

To Tim and Patty—you have helped me become your father. You have inspired me to see myself as Saint Joseph was to Jesus and as God the Father is to us.

To my parents and my brothers for your support and prayers. To Anne's parents and siblings for being by my side in my recoveries.

To Dr. Einhorn and the staff at Indiana University Medical Center for taking care of me. I would not be here today if it weren't for you.

To Monsignor Thomas Martin, a priest in our diocese of Kalamazoo, for teaching me about God's love as seen through Saint Teresa of Avila, Saint Therese of Lisieux, and Saint John of the Cross.

To my friends from college and medical school, neighbors, family friends, and my relatives for your prayers and for being so supportive in my care.

To my friends Joe Bower, Mark and Laura Eiler, and Donna Keller for looking at the manuscript and giving me your feedback. Your comments and suggestions for change have helped the book become what it is today.

To the staff at Archway Publishing for helping me with the editing, design, marketing, and publishing of this book.

To John Lacko Photography for doing the book photography.

# Notes

1  Ian Morgan Cron and Suzanne Stabile, *The Road Back to You: An Enneagram Journey to Self-Discovery* (InterVarsity Press, 2016).

2  James Martin, SJ, *Jesus: A Pilgrimage* (Harper One, 2014).

3  Fr. Peter John Cameron, ed., *Benedictus: Day by Day with Pope Benedict XVI* (Ignatius Press, 2006), 56, 325.

4  David Hazard, *A Day in Your Presence: A 40-Day Journey in the Company of Francis of Assisi* (Bethany House Publishers, 1992).

5  Dom Jean-Baptist Chautard, OCSO, *The Soul of the Apostolate* (Trappist, KY: The Abbey of Gethsemani, 1946).

6  Charles De Foucauld by Jean-Jacques Antier. Ignatius Press, 1999.

7  *Divine Intimacy* by Father Gabriel of St. Mary Magdalen, O.C.D. Tan Books and Publishers, 1996.

8  *An Introduction to the Devout Life* by St. Francis de Sales. Tan Books and Publishers, 1994.

9  *The Way of Perfection* by St. Teresa of Avila, translated by E. Allison Peers. Image Books, Doubleday, 1964

10  *The Interior Castle* by St. Teresa of Avila, translated by The Benedictines of Stanbrook and revised by Rev. Fr. Benedict Zimmerman, O.C.D. Tan Books and Publishers, 1997.

11  *The Sermon on the Mount, the Key to Success in Life* by Emmet Fox. HarperSanFrancisco, a division of Harper Collins Publishers, 1989.

12  *Merriam-Webster Dictionary*, 2019.

13  *St. Joseph & Daily Christian Living* by Francis L. Filas, SJ. The Macmillan Company, 1959.

14  *The Return of the Prodigal Son, A Story of Homecoming*, by Henri J.M. Nouwen. Image Books, Doubleday, 1994.

15  *The Passion of the Christ*, A Mel Gibson Film. Twentieth Century Fox Film, 2004.

16  Byers, Gary. "The Biblical Cities of Tyre and Sidon," Associates for
    Biblical Research, created January 26, 2010. Retrieved from https://www.
    biblearcheology.org

17  Mark, Joshua. "Canaan." Ancient History Encyclopedia, last modified
    October 23, 2018. Retrieved from http://www.ancient.eu/canaan/

18  *The Confessions by Saint Augustine of Hippo*, translated by Maria Boulding,
    O.S.B and edited by David Vincent Meconi, S.J. Ignatius Press, 2012.

19  *The Liturgy of the Hours*, Catholic Book Publishing Corp. 1975

20  The Magnificat, www.magnificat.com

21  *Benedictus, Day by Day with Pope Benedict XVI*. Ignatius Press/Magnificat,
    pages 56 and 325, 2006.

22  *Jesus, A Pilgrimage*, by James Martin, S.J. Harper One, 2014.

23  *Benedictus, Day by Day with Pope Benedict XVI*. Ignatius Press/Magnificat,
    page 198.

24  *The Impact of God, Soundings from St. John of the Cross*, by Iain Matthew.
    Hodder and Stoughton, a division of Hodder Headline Ltd, 1995.

25  *John of the Cross, Doctor of Light and Love*, by Kieran Kavanaugh. The
    Crossroad Publishing Company, 1999.

# About the Author

John J. Spitzer, M.D., a native of Salem, New Jersey, moved with his family to Cali, Colombia, at age six. After finishing elementary and high school in Colombia, he returned to the United States to pursue his education in medicine. He is a practicing pediatrician in private practice and also a clinical assistant professor in pediatric medicine at Western Michigan University Homer Stryker M.D. School of Medicine. He lives in Kalamazoo, Michigan, with his wife, Anne, and has two young adult children, Tim and Patty. He enjoys running, soccer, and reading.

CPSIA information can be obtained
at www.ICGtesting.com
Printed in the USA
LVHW041433131221
706069LV00017B/976

9 781665 704458